Lindsey Cowburn P2.

Access to A-Level History
General Editor: Keith Randell

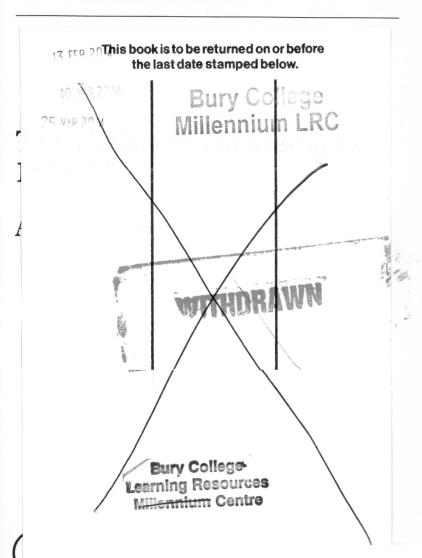

Edward Arnold

© Andrina Stiles 1986

First published in Great Britain 1986
by Edward Arnold (Publishers) Ltd
41 Bedford Square
London WC2 3DQ

Edward Arnold (Australia) Pty Ltd
80 Waverley Road
Caulfield East 3145
PO Box 234
Melbourne

British Library Cataloguing in Publication Data
Stiles, Andrina
   The unification of Germany 1815–90. –
   (Access to A-Level history)
   1. Germany – History – 1815–1866
   2. Germany – History – 1866–1871
   3. Germany – History – 1871–1918
   I. Title   II. Series
   943′.07   DD203

   ISBN 0–7131–7478–1

Text set in Linotron Plantin
by Northern Phototypesetting Co, Bolton
Printed and bound in Great Britain
by J. W. Arrowsmith Ltd, Bristol

Contents

Preface

To the teacher

The Access to A-Level History series has been planned with the A-Level student specifically in mind. The amount of factual detail is suitable for the requirements of A-Level, and care has been taken to ensure that all the 'facts' included have been explained or placed in context so as to allow proper understanding. Differing interpretations of events are discussed as appropriate and extracts from sources are woven into the main text. This is essential if A-Level students are to be encouraged to argue a case, bringing in suitable evidence to substantiate their points. The hope is that the text will be sufficiently interesting to increase student motivation towards reading history books, and sufficiently stimulating to encourage students to think analytically about what they have learnt.

It is also intended that the series will offer direct assistance to students in preparing to answer both essay and source-based questions. The sections providing guidance to the student which appear at the end of each chapter could be used either as a basis for class discussion or by students when working on their own. Direct help is also given with note making and realistic suggestions are made for further reading.

To the student

Many of you will find that this suggested procedure will enable you to derive the most benefit from each book:

1   Read the whole chapter as fast as you can, preferably in one sitting.
2   Study the flow diagram at the end of the chapter, ensuring that you understand the general pattern of events covered.
3   Study the 'Answering essay questions on . . .' section at the end of the chapter, consciously identifying the major issues involved.
4   Read the 'Making notes on . . .' section at the end of the chapter, and decide on the pattern of notes you will make.
5   Read the chapter a second time, stopping at each * or chapter sub-heading to make notes on what you have just read.
6   Attempt the 'Source-based questions on . . .' section.

When you have finished the book decide whether you need to do further reading on the topic. This will be important if you are seriously aspiring to a high grade at A-Level. The 'Further Reading' section at the end of the book will help you decide what to choose

I wish you well with your A-Level studies. I hope they are both enjoyable and successful. If you can think of any ways in which this book could be more useful to students please write to me with your suggestions.   Keith Randell

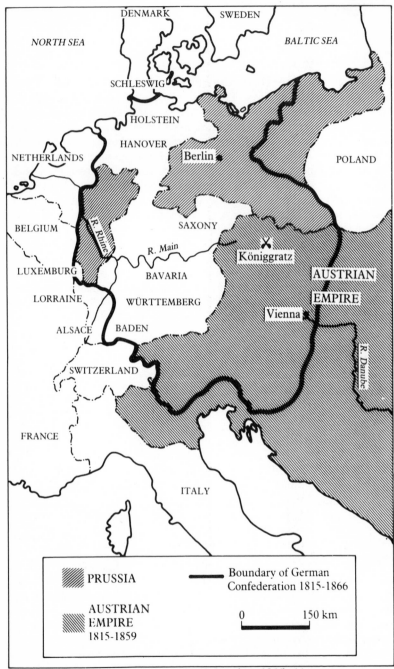

Austria, Prussia and the German Confederation, 1815–66

Introduction: The Unification of Germany, 1815–90

Before 1871 Germany did not exist as a country in the sense of being a unified political state. Throughout the Middle Ages and the early modern period (right up to the early nineteenth century) the area generally known as Germany was made up of hundreds of separate states that were virtually independent. These ranged from small city states and small areas of countryside ruled over by noblemen to large and powerful kingdoms, such as Prussia. In nominal control over the whole area was an Emperor – with the title of Holy Roman Emperor, a reflection of the claim to be the direct successor to the power of the Roman Emperors of ancient times. But the Emperor had little power, apart from that gained by having territories to rule over in his own right.

To make the situation more complicated, Germany lacked clear natural frontiers, especially in the east and in the south. It was not even possible to define its extent on ethnic grounds. In many areas the population was a mixture of German and Slav speakers such as Poles and Czechs, while some regions peopled almost entirely by Germans were cut off from their fellow German speakers by large communities of other ethnic groups. It did not even make sense to work by the boundaries of the Holy Roman Empire because these included much land peopled by French, Dutch, Danish, Polish and Czech speakers and excluded sizeable territories with a predominantly German population.

Each Holy Roman Emperor was elected to his position. It was therefore possible in theory for any family to supply an emperor, but in practice only members of the Habsburg family were chosen. They ruled extensive territories which centred on Austria. The Habsburg Empire – known as Austria or the Austrian Empire between 1815 and 1867, and as Austria–Hungary or the Dual Monarchy between 1867 and 1918 – included much of the southern part of what was known as Germany. The Habsburgs were Germans and their empire had been regarded as the leading German power for a long time before 1815.

In 1815 two German states were to be numbered among the five European Great Powers. The first and strongest was Austria. The second was the least important of the Great Powers – Prussia. By a series of annexations and marriages with heiresses Prussia had grown from relative insignificance to major power status in a little more than a century. Like Austria, she had suffered badly at the hands of Napoleon but she had recovered and her armies had played a large part in the eventual defeat of the French in 1813 and 1814.

Although it was not recognized at the time, the seeds were sown for a shift in the balance between the two German Powers in the Vienna

Settlement of 1815, which distributed territory at the end of the Napoleonic Wars. Whereas Austria acquired new possessions outside Germany (mainly in Italy), Prussia gained extensively in western Germany, and lost Polish lands to Russia, and in the process turned herself from being a state with interests mainly in eastern Germany to being the dominant power in the whole of the northern half of Germany. The events discussed in this book are mainly concerned with how this situation developed to produce the unitary political state of Germany.

The struggle between Austria and Prussia for mastery in Germany is not, however, the only theme that needs to be explored. There were many Germans at the time who did not see matters in terms of power politics. Even in 1815 there were tens of thousands of people, especially among the young, the educated, and the middle and upper classes, who felt passionately that Germans deserved to have a fatherland in the same way as the English and French already had. They longed for a united Germany to give visible form to their strongly-held sense of national identity. The numbers of these German nationalists grew greatly in the years after 1815. They came near to achieving their objective in 1848, but they failed. How and why they failed needs to be investigated.

Many of the early successes in bringing about a more united Germany were achieved in economic affairs rather than in the field of politics. It is important to understand what these were and to consider what part they played in shaping the form that unification eventually took.

Historians differ in their views on the relative importance of impersonal forces, such as economics, and the work of individuals in bringing about major changes in the past. The latter stages of German unification were dominated by one man, Otto von Bismarck. Some would argue that he masterminded the whole affair; others would say that he unscrupulously manipulated situations as they arose to gain an advantage for his state, Prussia. Others again would maintain that his actions were largely irrelevant because greater forces, especially of ideas and economics, were at work that would have ensured eventual unification whatever the politicians had done. The evidence allows each of these interpretations to be supported and we are left searching for the balance of probability.

The state of Germany came into existence in 1871. But although the new country was united in that it could be coloured the same shade on the map, in many important respects there was no unity. In the next 20 years Bismarck tried to extend the existing political unification. The problems he faced need to be understood and an assessment made of how far he was successful in solving them.

Thus five major issues need to be kept in mind as this book is read. Some are themes that appear throughout; others are restricted to particular sections. In both cases you might find it helpful to have a sheet of paper headed with wording that describes the issue so that major points can be noted down as they are identified. The flow diagram on page 5 will help you to understand the events that you are about to explore.

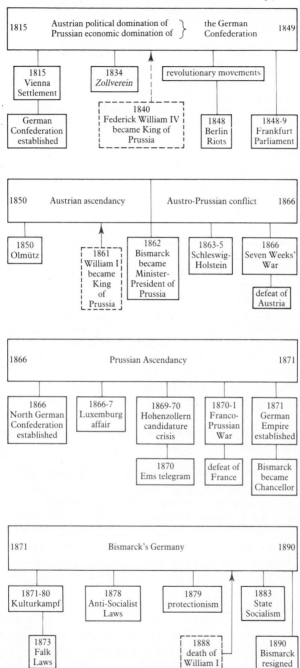

| 1815 | Austrian political domination of
Prussian economic domination of } | the German
Confederation | 1849 |

| 1815
Vienna
Settlement | 1834
Zollverein | revolutionary movements | |

| German
Confederation
established | 1840
Federick William IV
became King of
Prussia | 1848
Berlin
Riots | 1848-9
Frankfurt
Parliament |

| 1850 | Austrian ascendancy | Austro-Prussian conflict | 1866 |

| 1850
Olmütz | 1861
William I
became
King
of
Prussia | 1862
Bismarck
became
Minister-
President of
Prussia | 1863-5
Schleswig-
Holstein | 1866
Seven Weeks'
War |

defeat of
Austria

| 1866 | Prussian Ascendancy | 1871 |

| 1866
North German
Confederation
established | 1866-7
Luxemburg
affair | 1869-70
Hohenzollern
candidature
crisis | 1870-1
Franco-
Prussian
War | 1871
German
Empire
established |

| 1870
Ems telegram | defeat of
France | Bismarck
became
Chancellor |

| 1871 | Bismarck's Germany | 1890 |

| 1871-80
Kulturkampf | 1878
Anti-Socialist
Laws | 1879
protectionism | 1883
State
Socialism |

| 1873
Falk
Laws | 1888
death of
William I | 1890
Bismarck
resigned |

Summary – the unification of Germany, 1815–90

CHAPTER 1

Germany 1815–48

1 The German Confederation

At the end of the eighteenth century the centre of Europe was still occupied, as it had been since the Middle Ages, by the Holy Roman Empire. This was a collection of over 390 semi-independent states, most of them very tiny, loosely united under the nominal rule of the Holy Roman Emperor, who was also Emperor of Austria. Apart from Austria, only one state within the Empire had any real power or importance in domestic and international affairs, and that was Prussia. When first Austria in 1805 and then Prussia in 1806 were defeated by Napoleon I, the Empire collapsed.

The old hotchpotch of states was reorganized, small states were amalgamated, and the total number was reduced to 39. Napoleon formed Bavaria, Saxony, Baden and 14 of the other states into an association, called the Confederation of the Rhine. This Confederation was under direct French control, and the French legal system replaced the different laws and judicial procedures of the separate states. A small beginning had been made in the political and judicial unification of Germany.

After the devastating defeat by Napoleon in 1806 and the humiliating loss of a large part of her territory, Prussia was determined to recover her position as a leading German state by driving out the French. Impressed by French military successes, Prussia decided to copy what had been done in revolutionary France. Much of the reorganization of Prussia in the next decade was an imitation of French reforms. The army was reorganized and rebuilt to a high standard of military preparedness, the government was overhauled and modernized to provide a strong and efficient central authority, and a new system of education was introduced to encourage Prussian patriotic feeling among students.

Popular anti-French opinion encouraged King Frederick William III to overcome his natural indecisiveness and in January 1813 he made an alliance with Russia against France. The Russian and Prussian allied armies launched a campaign to drive Napoleon's forces back towards France. In June Austria also declared war on France and in October Napoleon was defeated at the Battle of Leipzig. The French lost 50 000 men and were forced back to the River Rhine. Within a few months the allied armies invaded France and forced Napoleon to abdicate.

a) *The Vienna Settlement*

The 39 German states varied greatly in size. The two largest and most important were Austria and Prussia, sometimes referred to as the Dual Powers. They dominated the remaining states and were obvious rival candidates for the control of any united Germany. Both were among the

Great Powers who had contributed to Napoleon's downfall and who drew up the peace treaty at the Congress of Vienna in 1815. Not surprisingly, both benefited substantially from the settlement.

Prussia gained considerable areas of territory, including part of Saxony and the valuable Rhineland, as well as Westphalia and Pomerania. This more than compensated for the loss of much of her Polish territory to Russia and meant that the population of the Kingdom of Prussia had been more than doubled to ten million.

The sudden increase in size brought problems, particularly with the Rhineland. There most of the population were Catholics, while nearly all Prussians were Protestant. The Rhinelanders resented being annexed to Prussia from which they were separated by more than 80 kilometres and with which they had little in common. Not only were there differences in religion but in customs and traditions as well. The industrialized Rhineland with its numerous towns was in contrast with rural Prussia. It had come under French influence as part of Napoleon's Confederation of the Rhine, and the inhabitants considered themselves part of western Europe and regarded the Prussians as an alien culture from the east.

Prussia had done as much if not more than Austria in driving the French out of Germany, but was able to exercise less influence at the Peace Congress. This was mainly because the Prussian delegation was handicapped in negotiations by the inconsistent policies of their King and his refusal to follow his ministers' advice. The most important influence on the future of the German states was that of Prince Metternich, who was Foreign Minister of Austria from 1809–48 and Chancellor (Chief Minister) from 1821–48.

Metternich's aim was the maintenance of Austria's traditional authority over the German states. He was not concerned with German political unity, and his negotiations ensured that Germany would become a loose confederation of states under Austrian control.

* In June 1815 the German Confederation or *Bund* was established with the aim of 'maintaining the external and internal security and the independence and integrity of the individual states'. Its declared aim was therefore the maintenance of the status quo in individual states through a system of mutual assistance in times of danger, such as internal rebellion or external aggression. It was not interested in or concerned with promoting a united Germany. In fact its aim was exactly the opposite, for none of the rulers of the separate states wished to see their independence limited by the establishment of a power organization covering the whole of Germany. Thus no objection was raised when the boundaries of the Confederation were modelled on those of the old Holy Roman Empire rather than on ones that would encourage the development of a nation state of Germany. So areas peopled by Poles, Czechs, Danes and French were included and provinces with largely German-speaking populations were excluded. States such as Luxemburg and Holstein which were

See Preface for explanation of * symbol.

ruled over by foreign monarchs were within the Confederation while large parts of German-speaking Austria and Prussia were not.

The Confederation had only one executive body, the *Bundestag* or Diet, which met at Frankfurt. This was a permanent conference of representatives, who were not elected but were sent by their governments with instructions how to act, and was presided over by the Austrian representative.

The Diet met for the first time at the end of 1816. It was soon clear that little would be achieved. For one thing the agreement of every state government was required before any measure could be passed. This total agreement was seldom forthcoming, for representatives were more concerned with safeguarding the interests and sovereignty of the states than working for the Confederation as a whole.

Each German state had its own independent ruler, its own government and its own army. The Confederation appointed ambassadors and could make foreign treaties on behalf of its members. Otherwise it had very little direct control over the individual states, apart from being able to prevent them making foreign alliances which might threaten the security of the Confederation, or concluding separate peace agreements in the event of the Confederation being involved in war. The Constitution of the Confederation, the Federal Act, had empowered the Diet to organize a Federal Army and to develop commercial and economic co-operation between the states, but local jealousies and fiercely guarded independence meant that nothing of importance was done to unify the Confederation militarily or economically.

One of the most important Articles of the Federal Act had laid down that the ruler of each state should sooner or later give his subjects a 'Constitution of Regional Estates'. Some states, including Austria and Prussia ignored the Article, but most of the small north German states, and some of the larger ones such as Hanover and Saxony allowed the 'estates' to meet. These 'estates' were traditional representative bodies, not always elected, and usually composed largely of nobles. In the south some states had written constitutions with elected assemblies which had the power to make laws and control taxation, but even in these states the assemblies had no direct part in government, for the ruler appointed his own ministers who were responsible only to him.

The Confederation was a very conservative organization, harking back in its political ideas to pre-Napoleonic times. It was little more than the ghost of the Holy Roman Empire. The old absolute government with all political power in the hands of the ruler had been restored in most of the individual states. In the years between 1818 and 1820 Bavaria, Baden, Württemberg and Hesse–Darmstadt introduced constitutions modelled on the French Charter of 1814, but the majority of rulers clung obstinately to their virtually absolute power. They agreed with the ideas of the Swiss writer, Haller, who declared that the state was the private property of the monarch. This was a very satisfactory creed from their point of view, and few of their subjects upset them by challenging it. Only among university students and teachers was there any real opposition.

2 Political Movements Working for Reform

Student societies with a strong political flavour had grown up in the universities in 1813 after the battle of Leipzig which drove the French out of the German states. The defeat of Napoleon was a great encouragement to nationalism, and the idea of an independent united Germany had an emotional appeal, particularly to many young university students, who tended to take up the cause in a romantic, passionate and impractical way.

Metternich exaggerated their importance, especially when in 1819 a member of an extreme student society murdered Kotzebu, a secret agent of the Russian Tsar. This murder prompted Metternich to take action. He consulted the King of Prussia and then summoned representatives of the German states to meet him at Carlsbad. Their decisions were ratified by the Diet as the Carlsbad Decrees. These provided inspectors for universities, student societies were disbanded, press censorship introduced and a commission set up to investigate so-called revolutionary movements. The Carlsbad Decrees included:

1 THE UNIVERSITY LAW
1. The Sovereign shall make choice for each university of an extraordinary commissioner, furnished with suitable instructions and powers, residing in the place where the university is
5 established . . .
The duty of this commissioner shall be to watch over the most rigorous observation of the laws and disciplinary regulations; to observe carefully the spirit with which the professors are guided in the scientific courses, or in the method of instruction, to give the
10 instruction a salutary direction, suited to the future destiny of the students, and to devote a constant attention to everything which may tend to the maintenance of morality, good order and decency among the youths . . .
2. The Governments of the States members of the confederation
15 reciprocally engage to remove from the universities . . . the professors and other public teachers against whom it may be proved that in departing from their duty, in overstepping the bounds of their duty, in abusing their legitimate influence over the minds of youth, by the propagation of pernicious dogmas, hostile
20 to order and public tranquillity . . .

THE PRESS LAW
As long as the present decree shall be in force, no daily paper or

pamphlet of less than twenty sheets shall be issued from the press without the previous consent of the public authority.

25 LAW ESTABLISHING A CENTRAL COMMISSION OF INVESTIGATION
1. Within fourteen days from the date of this decree, an extraordinary commission of enquiry, appointed by the Diet and composed of seven members, including the president, shall assemble in the city of Mainz . . .
30   2. The object of this commission is to make careful and detailed enquiries respecting the facts, the origin and the multifarious ramifications of the secret revolutionary activities and demagogic associations, directed against the political constitution and internal repose of the confederation . . .

As a result of the Decrees a number of Professors were dismissed from their posts. Reactionary forces had triumphed. In the following year, 1820, Metternich, suspicious of even the limited constitutions of the south German states, sought their abolition at the Congress of Troppau. He failed, but in 1821 he made it more difficult for liberal ideas to gain ground by persuading all the states to restrict the subjects which their assemblies could discuss.

* The liberal ideas which Metternich so distrusted were concerned with constitutional reform and the replacing of an absolute and autocratic government by a parliamentary system firmly based on the rule of law. Liberals spoke of human rights and freedoms – freedom of speech, freedom of the press, freedom of worship, freedom to form political associations and freedom to hold political meetings. Their ideas on parliamentary representation were restricted to giving the vote to men of property. There was no question of a universal franchise, for liberals were almost exclusively well-educated, well-to-do members of the middle class concerned with their own economic and political interests and not with radical changes in the structure of society. Liberals disliked excesses of any kind, were generally opposed to violence and hoped to achieve their aims by intellectual argument and peaceful persuasion. Too often, though, talk became a substitute for action.

* Many liberals were also nationalists, but not all nationalists were liberals. Some nationalists held much more extreme republican or revolutionary political views. In the late eighteenth century nationalism (the belief in a national identity) became merged with the idea of an independent state with fixed geographical boundaries and its own government. The national identity could be based on some or all the elements of a common race, language, culture, religion or geographical area.

In some countries where all or most of these elements were present, strong nationalist movements developed quickly and successfully. In Germany there was no religious unity; the south and west were mainly Catholic and the north Lutheran Protestant. There were no clearly defined frontiers either, but there was a common language and a shared cultural tradition based on a literary and artistic heritage. In addition there was felt to be a racial bond uniting all Germans, and this was to become more important over the years.

The seeds of German nationalism had been sown by the philosopher, Herder, before the end of the eighteenth century. He had taught that all people or races had their own special and unique spirit, which made them different from neighbouring peoples. People living in different areas of the world developed in different ways and produced their own culture, tradition, customs and way of life. These cultures should be cherished and developed as the basis for a national identity. Herder's ideas of a cultural basis for nationhood were taken up and expanded by others, the most important of whom was Hegel, a professor in the University of Berlin, who died in 1831. He taught that man only achieved his full potential as a human being by service to the state. As an individual he was nothing, as part of a national community he was everything. On his own he could not be a true German; he needed to find his identity as a German by being part of a German nation.

It is difficult to know how far these liberal and nationalist ideas filtered down from the educated minority to the rest of the population. The years between 1815 and 1848 are often called the *Vormärz* (literally Pre-March). German historians have given them this name because they regard them as a prelude to the March revolutions in Berlin in 1848. The *Vormärz* years were certainly a time of political excitement. Much of it was of an intellectual and theoretical kind, but lectures, debates, books and pamphlets, which put forward the new ideas, reached only a limited audience.

In some cases, however, the message was carried to the workers in the cities by well-meaning liberals who set up study groups, and groups were sometimes formed by workers themselves, particularly among printers. Some of the groups were large with several hundred members, like those in Hamburg, and they discussed politics and planned revolution, or at least strike action. Their politics became democratic rather than liberal, centred on the sovereignty of the people rather than on the sovereignty of parliament, on a republic rather than a monarchy, and on violence rather than on peaceful means to obtain their ends. However enthusiastic and active these groups were, they involved only a small proportion of workers in the cities and the workers on the land hardly at all. Liberalism and nationalism remained largely middle class before 1848.

3 Metternich

The development of these two movements made Metternich extremely uneasy about the future of the German Confederation. If allowed to go unchecked, they could only lead to the overthrow of absolute governments in the individual states and to demands for a united Germany, with national and state representative assemblies. These demands might be at the moment only the noisy, clamour of a few 'intellectuals' and workers, but the danger was that they could become the basis of popular revolution.

Metternich believed that the maintenance of international peace was directly linked with the prevention of revolution in individual states. Internal and international affairs were inseparable. What happened inside one state was of concern to other states, and entitled them to intervene if they considered it necessary. There was an equilibrium or balance inside each state, where the social order had to be defended against the forces of destruction. For Metternich these forces were nationalism and liberalism. He therefore set his face against any constitutional change, however modest, for the salvation of society depended on the preservation of the monarchy and respect for the nobility. Monarchs should therefore join together to save society from subversive revolution.

a) *The Congress of Troppau*

The Vienna Settlement of 1815 had restored many of the monarchs of Europe to their thrones and Metternich was determined that they should be kept there. He developed the idea of European Congresses, meetings of the Great Powers to discuss and settle international disagreements and maintain peace. Four such Congresses were held between 1818 and 1822 and at one of them, the Congress of Troppau in 1820, discussion centred on revolutions which had broken out in Spain, Portugal, Piedmont, and Naples. All of these states had demanded constitutions from their rulers. During the Congress, Metternich sent a secret memorandum to the Tsar of Russia:

1　Kings have to calculate the chances of their very existence in the immediate future; passions are let loose, and league together to overthrow everything which society respects as the basis of its existence; religion, public morality, laws, customs, rights, and
5　duties, all are attacked, confounded, overthrown, or called into question. The great mass of the people are tranquil spectators of these attacks and revolutions, and of the absolute want of all means of defence. A few are carried off by the torrent, but the wishes of the immense majority are to maintain a repose which exists no
10　longer, and of which even the first elements seem to be lost . . .

　　. . . The agitated classes are principally composed of wealthy men – real cosmopolitans, securing their personal advantage at the expense of any order of things whatever – paid State officials, men of letters, lawyers, and the individuals charged with the public
15　education.

　　To those classes may be added that of the falsely ambitious, whose number is never considerable among the lower orders, but is larger in the higher ranks of society.

There is besides scarcely any epoch which does not offer a
20 rallying cry to some particular faction. This cry, since 1815, has been Constitution. But do not let us deceive ourselves: this word, susceptible of great latitude of interpretation, would be but imperfectly understood if we supposed that the factions attached quite the same meaning to it under the different régimes. Such is
25 certainly not the case. In pure monarchies it is qualified by the name of 'national representation'. In countries which have lately been brought under the representative régime it is called 'development', and promises charters and fundamental laws. Everywhere it means change and trouble.
30   We are convinced that society can no longer be saved without strong and vigorous resolutions on the part of the Governments still free in their opinions and actions. . . . The first principle to be followed by the monarchs, united as they are by the coincidence of their desires and opinions, should be that of maintaining
35 the stability of political institutions against the disorganised excitement which has taken possession of men's minds; the immutability of principles against the madness of their interpretation; and respect for laws actually in force against a desire for their destruction. . . . In short, let the great monarchs strengthen their
40 union, and prove to the world that if it exists, it is beneficent, and ensures the political peace of Europe; that it is powerful only for the maintenance of tranquillity at a time when so many attacks are directed against it; that the principles which they profess are paternal and protective, menacing only disturbers of public tran-
45 quillity.

The Tsar was in sympathy with Metternich's beliefs, and put forward a proposal at the Congress that the Great Powers of Russia, Austria and Prussia should agree to act jointly, using force if necessary, to restore any government which had itself been overthrown by force. The proposal was accepted and the three Great Powers announced jointly, in the Protocol of Troppau, that they 'would never recognize the rights of a people to restrict the powers of their King'. This ran directly contrary to the ambitions of liberals and nationalists everywhere, and was particularly disappointing to those in the German states. Prussia as well as Austria was firmly ranged on the side of reaction.

As well as the weapons of diplomacy and threats of force, Metternich used those of the police state to maintain the status quo. A special office was set up in Vienna to open, copy and then reseal foreign correspondence passing through Austria. This gave him an enormous amount of secret information about the activities of other governments and it was backed up by reports from his network of spies and secret agents throughout Europe and by the work of his secret police.

By a combination of repression and press censorship in individual states, and a system of international alliances to preserve peace, Metternich hoped to keep Europe quiet and to allow revolutionary fervour to simmer down. Throughout the 1820s he was generally successful.

★ In the 1830s the picture changed. The July Revolution in Paris in 1830 sparked off demonstrations and riots in several south German states. The demands were for a constitution as laid down in the Federal Act of 1815, which had set up the Confederation, or, if a constitution already existed, for its liberalization. In Brunswick the Duke was driven out and his successor was forced to grant a more liberal constitution. In both Saxony and Hesse-Cassel similar concessions were obtained. In Bavaria, Baden and Württemberg, where constitutions already existed, liberal opposition parties gained parliamentary seats in new elections, and greater freedom of the press allowed criticisms of the government. In Hanover the King granted a constitution in 1832 (although it was abolished five years later by his successor).

In the early 1830s a number of republican groups were busy with plans for the immediate unification of Germany. In 1832 25 000 nationalists met at the Hambach Festival in Bavaria to drink, talk and plan revolution. Metternich, not surprisingly, was thrown into a panic. In the same year with Prussian support, he persuaded the Diet to pass the Six Articles. These increased its control over the internal affairs of individual states, and, in particular, its control of the universities and the press. The effect was to make the Diet hated by nationalists everywhere in the Confederation, and in 1833 an armed student rising tried to take it over. The rising was quickly defeated and the Diet set up a special commission to round up young student agitators, many of whom were forming themselves into a 'Young Germany' movement. This movement was dedicated to establishing a united Germany based on liberal principles, international peace and free love. Faced with such developments, Metternich again summoned representatives from the Confederation to meet him in Vienna in 1834 to discuss the need for yet sterner action against subversive elements.

The years of political discussions and planning by liberals and nationalists during the 1820s and 1830s had achieved almost nothing, for they were powerless against Metternich's domination. Certainly the Diet would do nothing to aid the liberal or nationalist causes, for it was now little more than the Austrian machinery of government within the Confederation, and as long as Prussia remained Austria's ally and equally reactionary, there was little hope of a change in the situation.

★ The 1840s, however, were to bring new and hopeful developments. In the south-western states the liberals increased their popular support and in Baden half the elected members of the Lower House of Parliament were government officials who had been converted to liberalism. When two of them were suspended in 1843, it led to a vote of no confidence in the government and its eventual defeat. Three years later the liberals in Baden managed to obtain a relaxation of press censorship, and reforms of the police and of the judicial system. In Hesse-Darmstadt there were strong liberal parliamentary campaigns for changes in electoral rules and for a free press. In Bavaria the liberals were helped by an unexpected change of policy on the part of the half-mad King, Ludwig I. His passion for a dancer led him to propose that she should be given a title and land and be introduced to court. When his advisers criticized him, he dismissed the government and replaced his reactionary ministers with liberal ones.

In Prussia the King, Frederick William III, who had ruled as an absolute monarch for over forty years, died in 1840. He had avoided granting a constitution, partly because it was against his inclination to do so, and partly because he had been heavily pressurized by Austria. He had close ties with Austria, through Prussia's association with the Protocol of Troppau, and through his foreign minister, a friend of Metternich's.

He was succeeded by his son Frederick William IV, whose policies were to fluctuate widely throughout his reign. Sometimes he behaved as a reactionary absolutist, sometimes as a constitutional monarch. He started by acting as many liberals wished him to. He released many political prisoners, abolished censorship and appointed a leading liberal to the Council of State. In 1842 he arranged for the Prussian provincial Diets to elect representatives to meet as an advisory body on a temporary basis in Berlin. He extended slightly the powers of the provincial Diets and allowed them to publish reports of their debates.

Encouraged by this, middle-class liberals in the Rhineland immediately began to agitate for a constitution and the calling of a single Diet or Parliament for all Prussian territories. The conservative landed aristocracy of Prussia, the *Junkers*, watched the activities of the King with anxiety and even considered a coup to replace him with his brother, William.

Frederick William, taking fright at finding himself under political attack from both left and right, reimposed press censorship in 1843. In 1847 he called a meeting of the United Diet in Berlin to vote a loan for building a railway to link East Prussia and Berlin. Liberal hopes that this was the fulfilment of their demand for a single Diet for all Prussia were soon dashed, for the United Diet refused to grant the loan for the railway and was soon dispersed. The liberals renewed their demands for a national assembly of the kind promised in the Vienna Settlement, but the king refused. He would go no further towards granting a constitution.

In 1847 liberal and nationalist sentiments found expression in the foundation at Heidelberg of a newspaper with the prophetic title of *Die Deutsche Zeitung* (The German Newspaper). Equally important was a meeting of liberal representatives of the south-western states at Hippenheim. They drew up a programme of reform, demanded an elected national Diet and detailed their complaints which were published in *Die Deutsche Zeitung*:

1　The Diet has so far not fulfilled the tasks set it by the Act of the Confederation in the fields of representation by estates, free trade, communications, navigation, freedom of the press etc; the federal defence regulation provides neither for the arming of the
5　population nor for a uniformly organised federal force. On the contrary the press is harassed by censorship; the discussions of the Diet are enveloped in secrecy. . . . The only expression of the common German interests in existence, the Customs Union, was not created by the Confederation, but negotiated outside its
10　framework, through treaties between individual states; negotiations about a German law on bills of exchange, and about a postal union, are conducted not by the Confederation but by the several governments. . . .
　　The liberation of the press . . . , open and oral judicial
15　proceedings with juries, separation of the executive and judicial powers, transfer to the courts of the administration of the laws . . . , drafting of a police criminal code, freeing the soil and its tillers from medieval burdens, independence of the communes in the administration of their affairs, reduction of the cost of the
20　standing army and establishments of a national guard etc. were discussed at length, as were the constitutional means that could be used to give force to the just demands of the people. Particular attention was given to possible ways of reducing impoverishment and want and, a closely related topic, of reforming the system of
25　taxation. . . .

4 Economic Developments

Few liberals would have foreseen at any time during the years between 1815 and 1848 that the nationalist aim of the political unification of Germany would eventually be brought about by Prussia, one of the most reactionary of the German states, nor if they had, would they have been best pleased by the manner of its doing. Nevertheless, the basis for the unification of Germany had already been laid by Prussia before 1840, and that basis, which was not political but economic, was the *Zollverein* or Prussian Customs Union.

In the ten years after the Treaty of Vienna, there was very little industry in Germany. Its development was hampered by the customs barriers between the 39 States of the Confederation. This made internal trade very slow and expensive and greatly complicated the lives of businessmen and merchants. Even within a single state there were large numbers of tolls. Variations in currency values within the Confederation was an added problem. The silver thaler, the main unit of coinage, varied in value from state to state.

In 1818 Rhineland manufacturers complained to the King of Prussia about the massive burden on home industry, and about competition from unrestricted foreign imports, on which no duty was charged. As a result, in the same year, the Prussian Tariff Reform Law brought into being the Prussian Customs Union (later to become the *Zollverein*). The law did away with the web of internal customs duties and replaced them by a tariff to be charged at the Prussian state frontier. The tariff was low: nothing at all on raw materials, an average of 10 per cent on manufactured goods and 20 per cent on luxury goods such as sugar or tea. High tariffs would only have encouraged smuggling, which was already widespread, and, in any case, Prussia was not economically or politically strong enough to engage in a tariff war with other countries, who would only have put high duties on Prussian exports, particularly corn and linen, in return.

Later Prussia did introduce customs duties on raw materials, especially iron and cotton yarn imported from Britain, for as time went on the Union became more protectionist, as it set out to further protect home industry from foreign competition by increasing import duties on foreign goods. At the same time it was working to extend free trade, first within Prussia and then within other states in the Confederation, by getting rid of as many internal trade barriers as possible so goods would move more freely. This meant wider markets for home produced goods at cheaper prices. As part of these policies, the Union put a heavy tax on any foreign manufactured goods simply passing through Prussian territory.

After 1815 the Prussian Government had quickly realized the need to industrialize. In 1821 a Trades Institute was set up to encourage industry and to design and produce new machines for factories. Prussian trade benefited from taking over the good network of roads in the Rhineland which the French had built during the occupation. Communications were improved again when the Prussian government branched out into railway building, and when steamboat services were introduced on the Rivers Rhine, Weser and Elbe.

In the early 1820s, soon after the foundation of the Prussian Customs Union, some of Prussia's smaller neighbours were so impressed by its economic success that they agreed to join a customs union with Prussia, and even allowed Prussian customs officers into their territories to operate the system. In 1828 one of the larger neighbouring states, Hesse-Darmstadt, also signed a customs treaty with Prussia.

By 1830 customs unions were proliferating. As well as the Prussian–Hesse-Darmstadt union with its satellite neighbours in attendance there were two others. One was between Bavaria and Württemberg, and the other, known as the Middle German Commercial Union, was made up of Hanover, Brunswick, Saxony and several smaller states.

This Union was not quite like the others, for it was not so much concerned with encouraging its own trade as spoiling that of Prussia. Prussia was geographically well placed to control north-south routes through north Germany and to generate a large income out of duties charged on foreign goods carried along these routes. The Middle Union worked to protect and keep open the existing roads from the North Sea ports to the central German cities of Frankfurt and Leipzig and to build a series of new roads which would go round the states of the Prussian Customs Union. In this scheme they were thwarted by the Prussian Finance Minister, who encouraged the building of roads joining Prussia directly with Bavaria, Wüttemberg and Frankfurt. He also extended Prussian trade along the Rhine through a customs agreement with the Dutch.

a) The *Zollverein*

In 1830 Hesse-Cassel, one of the smaller but vitally important states of the Middle Union, ran into financial difficulties and revolutionary upheavals. The following year she joined the Prussian Customs union to the horror of her Middle Union partners. The Middle Union, which was already in trouble, collapsed soon after, while the Prussian Customs Union went from strength to strength.

In 1834 Bavaria and Württemberg joined the Prussians, and this new enlarged Customs Union, the *Zollverein*, covered 18 states. In 1836 when Baden and Frankfurt joined as well, the *Zollverein* included 25 states with a population of 26 million. It promised for all member states a common system of customs and tariffs, and the abolition of all internal customs barriers. Each state had the right to appoint some officials to the customs departments of other states, and as long as they did not break the rules of the *Zollverein* each state could negotiate its own trade treaties. The organization and supervision of the *Zollverein* was carried out by a specially appointed body, the *Zollverein* Congress. In the next few years a start was made on unifying both the currency and the system of weights and measures in the states of the *Zollverein*. The railways were greatly extended to make a quick and efficient means of communication between *Zollverein* members.

The experiment of the *Zollverein* had been successful. The member states had worked together, and Prussia had achieved a position of economic leadership within the Confederation. There had been a few difficulties: administration did not always work smoothly, and as any member state could veto a proposal at the *Zollverein* Congress, decisions were often held up or not made at all. The situation improved later, after 1866, when the rules were changed and a simple majority became enough to pass a measure. In the meantime the *Zollverein* became a focal point for national feeling, and when in 1844 it signed a favourable trade treaty with Belgium, it could be said to speak for the major part of the Confederation in international economic affairs.

The example of economic co-operation between the German states encouraged the liberals and nationalists. It made their dreams of a politically united Germany seem more likely to be realized. On a practical level the states of the *Zollverein* had prospered – would not the same be true following political unity? They pointed out the savings which could be made by doing away with 39 separate states, governments, legal systems, administrations and embassies, and replacing them with a central government.

Unfortunately, it was not as simple as that. In the 1840s many difficulties still stood in the way of a united Germany. There were religious tensions between the Catholic south and the Protestant north and economic divisions between the industrialized Rhineland and the rest of the states. In addition there was no clear agreement on what the frontiers of a united Germany should be. Support was divided between proposals for a *Kleindeutschland* (Little Germany) and for a *Grossdeutschland* (Large Germany). A *Kleindeutsch* solution would exclude Austria from a united Germany and make Prussia the dominant state: a *Grossdeutsch* solution would include Austria and leave her in a very strong position to assume the leadership of a united Germany.

The emotional appeal of nationalism was experienced by rapidly increasing numbers of Germans during the 1820s and 1830s. It was inflamed by poetry, music, history and philosophy, based on the twin themes of hatred of France and a highly coloured view of Germany's great, as yet unfulfilled role in Europe. It was fuelled by several situations in which foreign governments appeared to threaten Germany as a whole, and which made many Germans, who were normally content to think of themselves as Prussians, Bavarians, Hessians or members of other states, discontented that Germany could not speak with a single, strong voice at times of crisis. These feelings were particularly widespread in 1840 when it seemed likely that France would invade the German states along the Rhine in an attempt to force the other major powers to bow to her wishes over the Near Eastern Crisis involving the partial dismemberment of the Ottoman Empire. In the end France backed down, but not before much nationalistic feeling had been generated throughout Germany in the face of a threat from the 'old enemy'.

It is easy for us to understand why a threat from France should evoke such a response. After all, only 25 years had elapsed since the final defeat of Napoleon. Less immediately understandable is the reaction to a threat from Denmark, which was relatively small, weak and internationally insignificant. Yet in 1846 Denmark did as much to create support for the idea of German unification as had France in 1840. Immediately to the south of Denmark proper lay the duchies of Schleswig and Holstein. They were ruled over by the King of Denmark and were a part of his kingdom in all but name. Holstein had an overwhelmingly German-speaking population and was one of the member states of the German Confederation. When it seemed that the King of Denmark was about to incorporate Schleswig and Holstein into his kingdom, the outcry throughout Germany was enormous. What to most people throughout Europe, including the King of Denmark, seemed merely legal technicality was viewed by most Germans as a violation of the Fatherland to be resisted by force if need be. This strength of feeling was enough to persuade the King of Denmark to abandon his plans.

What was Prussia's aim in setting up the *Zollverein*? Successive Prussian Finance Ministers realized that doing away with internal customs duties, first within Prussia, and then between Prussia and neighbouring states, would increase trade and bring prosperity. It would also help unite Prussia with her distant Rhineland territories. As early as 1830, even before the *Zollverein* was formed, the Prussian Finance Minister had pointed out to his King that such a free trade organization would not only bring prosperity to Prussia and her associates, but would isolate Austria. This isolation would not only be economic but would eventually weaken her political influence within the Confederation. Many modern historians support the view that from the 1830s onwards Prussia was using the *Zollverein* to achieve 'a Prussian solution to the German question'. The argument is that those who found financial advantage in an economic union under Prussian leadership might be expected to take a favourable view of similar arrangements in a political union. The *Zollverein* was a force for unity in the 1840s and therefore a focal point for nationalist sentiments. As a result, Prussia, despite her reactionary political sympathies, came to be regarded by many as the natural leader of a united Germany.

Why did Austria stay outside the *Zollverein*? She had refused to join at the beginning, because she disagreed with the policy of free trade, unrestricted by customs barriers, as a way of extending trade and finding new markets. Austria's policy was protectionist. She already had large markets within the Austrian Empire for her home produced goods, and therefore, wanted high import duties to protect her industries and markets from cheap foreign imports. Joining the *Zollverein* would have meant reducing her import duties to the same level as the other states, and this she would not consider. Only if the *Zollverein* raised the general level of tariffs would Austria join, and this Prussia in turn would not consider. Austria gave Prussia a great opportunity when she refused to join. Prussia took it, established her position of leadership, and made sure that Austria would stay outside.

By 1848, if Austria still retained political control of the Confederation, Prussia had the economic leadership. The struggle between the two powers was to develop during the coming decade and was only to be resolved by war.

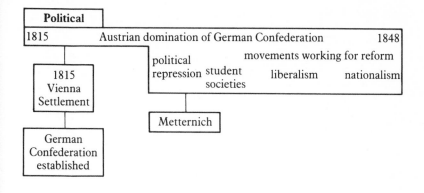

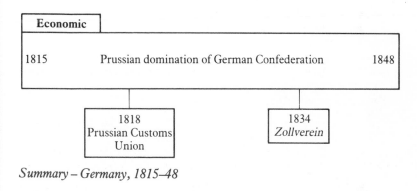

Summary – Germany, 1815–48

Making notes on 'Germany 1815–1848'

Your notes on this chapter should help you understand how the German Confederation of 1815 was organized and the roles of Austria and Prussia within it. You should also have a framework to discuss the importance of nationalism and the *Zollverein* in promoting the idea of German unification.

The following headings and subheadings should help you make clear notes:

1.   The German Confederation
1.1. The situation before 1815
1.2. The Vienna Settlement
1.3. The enlargment of Prussia
1.4. The German Confederation
2.   Political movements working for reform
2.1. Student societies

Answering essay questions on 'Germany, 1815–48'

Much of the material dealt with in this chapter will be used in answering general questions on the unification of Germany. Such questions are discussed on page 105.

The one topic from the period 1815–48 which tends to appear in A-Level questions as a fairly self-contained issue is the *Zollverein*. The approach adopted is to ask about its formation and the reasons for it (causes), and the effects it had, especially on the unification of Germany (consequences).

Typical examples of such questions are:

> In what ways did the *Zollverein* contribute to the economic and political development of Germany? (Oxford, 1983)
> Examine the causes of the formation of the *Zollverein* and its results for Prussia, Austria, and the German states. (Cambridge, 1982)

Make a list of the points you would use to explain a) the causes, and b) the consequences of the *Zollverein*. Keep the list and add to it once you have read chapter 3. Look at the points on your list. For each one decide whether the words 'economic' or 'political' describe it best. Put 'E' or 'P' against each one. Where you are tempted to put down both 'E' and 'P', rethink the point and if possible divide it into two. By grouping the 'E' and 'P' points together you should have ready a four part plan to answer an essay question such as:

> 'Examine the causes and consequences of the *Zollverein*.'

Source-based questions on 'Germany 1815–48'

1   The Carlsbad Decrees, 1819
Read carefully the extracts from the Carlsbad Decrees, given on page 9. Answer the following questions:
a)   In the University Law, the extraordinary commissioners are given four major duties. Summarize them briefly in your own words.

b) What are the implications of the phrase, 'suited to the future destiny of the students' (line 10)?

c) What can be learnt about the values and attitudes of the framers of the Carlsbad Decrees from the second article of the University Law?

d) The Press Law applied to daily papers and pamphlets of less than 20 sheets – why to these categories of publications in particular?

e) What was it hoped that the extraordinary commission of enquiry (line 26) would achieve?

2   Metternich's memorandum to Alexander I, 1820

Read carefully the extracts from Metternich's secret memorandum to Alexander I, given on page 12. Answer the following questions:

a) What does Metternich mean when he uses the phrases 'falsely ambitious' (line 16); 'pure monarchies' (line 25); and, 'the immutability of principles' (line 36)?

b) Summarize in a short paragraph the action which Metternich is urging Alexander to take.

c) Metternich argues that there must be no change in political institutions. What arguments does he use to support his point of view?

d) Alexander I was known to be an idealist with a strong sense of duty. What evidence does the memorandum contain to suggest that Metternich was attempting to appeal to this aspect of his character?

e) What were the implications of this memorandum for the development of the movement favouring German unification?

3   The Hippenheim Programme, 1847

Read carefully the extracts from the report of the Hippenheim meeting in *Die Deutsche Zeitung*, given on page 16. Answer the following questions.

a) Is the Diet mainly criticized for what it has done or for what it has not done?

b) What complaints are made about military matters? What suggestions are made for improvements in the situation?

c) What evidence does the report contain to suggest that those who met at Hippenheim were German nationalists?

d) What evidence does the report contain to suggest that those who met at Hippenheim belonged to the middle classes?

e) What do the extracts suggest about the interests and attitudes of the writer of the report?

CHAPTER 2

Germany in Revolution, 1848–49

1 Causes of Revolutionary Movements

1848 was a year to remember in Europe, a year of dramatic, violent events, of hope and of failure. It was the year of death in the cholera epidemic, which swept across Europe from Asia, causing such loss of life that for a while society in many areas was totally disorganized. It was the year of birth in the publication of Karl Marx's *Communist Manifesto*. This did not have the drama of the cholera epidemic and attracted little attention at the time, but in twenty years its message had spread across Europe and beyond to become, a century later, the basis of the political system of half the world. It began as a year of hope in the revolutions which broke out all over Europe. But it ended as a year of failure.

The revolutions were widespread, in France, in the German Confederation, in the Habsburg lands including Austria and Hungary, and in Italy. At first the revolutions seemed very successful. Even Metternich, the apparently immovable senior statesman of Europe, was forced into exile by events in Vienna, and in France Louise-Philippe lost his throne.

Why did these revolutions all happen in the same year? Historians used to think that the French troubles, which began in February 1848, simply triggered off copy-cat revolutions in other countries. Now the generally accepted view is that the revolutions took place at about the same time because conditions in France, Germany and the Austrian Empire were all very similar. These conditions, economic and social, were of the kind which give rise to revolutions.

* Since the middle of the previous century important changes had occurred in Europe. The population had grown dramatically, towns had increased in size and number, and industry had developed out of all recognition. Life in 1848 was very different from what it had been in 1748.

The reasons why the population doubled in the century up to 1848 are not certain. Economic historians can only say that it was more probably due to a declining death rate than to an increasing birth rate. In Prussia the population in the countryside increased by nearly 75 per cent between 1815 and 1848. Many people left the land and drifted to the towns in search of work or went to other parts of the world. Of the quarter of a million who left Germany in 1840s, most went to the United States in search of land and food.

* Those who remained in the countryside found life very hard. In eastern Prussia much of the land belonged to the *Junkers*, the landowning military aristocracy, and was worked by landless peasants. Even in the parts of Germany where the peasants had become tenant farmers rents were very high. It was difficult to make a living.

In 1846 and 1847 the corn harvests were disastrous and the situation was made worse by a serious outbreak of potato blight. Potatoes were the main item of diet for most German peasants, and failure of the crop meant starvation. There was distress and unrest, and food riots broke out. There had been poor harvests before, but the increased population made the position worse.

* The towns, especially the industrial towns, also felt the pressure on food supplies, and there was a sharp rise in food prices. Cereal prices increased by nearly 50 per cent in 1847. The cost of living rose steeply for everyone, but the workers suffered most, particularly those in the textile mills. The textile industry was going through difficult times. A recession started in 1847 and wages were cut. Higher prices and lower wages coincided and the workers' standard of living fell. Cheap alcohol gave some comfort in a hard life, and contemporary writers describe the great increase in drunkenness, especially among women and children factory workers.

Even in good times the workers did not live well. They were poorly clothed and inadequately fed. From the mid 1840s there was unemployment in many industries. One observer reported that unemployed factory workers were living worse than prisoners in dirty, damp and overcrowded accommodation, often twenty people to a room, six or seven to a bed. When work was available, working conditions were grim. The machines, especially in the textile factories, were not designed with the workers in mind. Men, women and children worked for 13 or more hours a day, often in cramped and awkward positions, crouched over the machines. This led to deformities of one kind or another among many of the workers. Men and women of 30 were already old.

* In both town and country, among workers and peasants, there was growing unrest. Dissatisfied with the existing state of affairs, they began to make demands. They wanted a better life for themselves and their families with enough food, reasonable housing, a shorter working day and improved working conditions. Their demands were clear, limited, practical and basically non-political. In fact they were, with few exceptions, not concerned with politics and political theories; they were only interested in the kind of government they had in so far as it affected their daily lives.

There were exceptions, of course. In towns like Cologne and Bonn the skilled craftsmen had their own trade organizations, and kept themselves apart from the unskilled factory workers, whom they both despised and feared. These skilled workers were articulate and politically aware. During 1848 they staged demonstrations, and elected representative assemblies to discuss their grievances. The assembly, or congress, held at Frankfurt drew up an Industrial Code to regulate hours of work, rates of pay and so on. (They later presented the Code to the Frankfurt Parliament for approval but it was turned down). At the time of the riots in Berlin in March 1848 some politically active workers organized themselves into Workers' Committees, demanding among other things the formation of trades unions, free education and a guaranteed minimum wage.

For Karl Marx and his supporters these events showed the development of a 'working class consciousness'. By this they meant that the workers had realized that, because the middle and upper classes owned the means of production (factories, mills, mines etc.), they must unite together in revolution to change this if they were to improve the quality of their lives. Some historians believe that the revolutions of 1848 orginated with the workers, and certainly they were the ones who fought and died in the streets behind the barricades; but it was not only the workers who made the revolutions. Others played an important part, particularly the educated middle classes.

 * The middle classes in Germany were suffering from frustration. There were not enough jobs to go round for the men qualified to become doctors, lawyers, teachers and civil servants. Career opportunities were limited, particularly in the civil service where all the senior posts were filled by members of the nobility. They were frustrated too by their lack of power, for in 1848 power lay where it always had, with the nobility. They owned the land, filled senior government jobs, officered the army, and guarded their privileges jealously against any infiltration by the middle classes.

The new political ideas of liberalism and nationalism, which were developing during the first half of the nineteenth century, proved very attractive to the dissatisfied middle classes (see page 10). By 1847 patriotism was running high, and the feelings of many Germans were expressed in a memorandum written by Prince Hohenlohe:

1   In the history of every nation there is an epoch in which it comes to full self consciousness and claims liberty to determine its own destiny. . . . We Germans have reached this stage. The nation demands a share in public administration as never before. . . . No
5   one will deny that it is hard on an energetic thinking man to be unable to say abroad 'I am a German' – not to be able to pride himself that the German flag is flying from his vessel, to have no German consul in case of emergency, but have to explain 'I am a Hessian, a Darmstädter, a Bückeburger; my fatherland was once
10 a great and powerful country, now it is shattered into nine and thirty splinters.'

2 Constitutional Movements

In the end the impetus for a German national revolution came surprisingly from the small, and hitherto undistinguished state of Baden in south-west Germany. There was already in Baden a constitution with a representative assembly elected on a wider franchise than in any other German state, and the people of Baden were more politically conscious than elsewhere in Germany. For years before 1847 the liberal politicians of Baden had been proposing a united Germany instead of the loose Confederation. Now they put their views forcefully to an assembly of liberals from all the south-west German states. (see page 15). This assembly, which met in October 1847, agreed on the urgent need for an independent German People's Parliament.

While this meeting was going on, radical politicians were holding their own meetings in south-west Germany, and again proceedings were dominated by the representatives from Baden. The radicals wanted fairer taxation, education for all, a people's army, better relations between employees and workers, and most important, the establishment of a united German Republic.

* The dramatic news of revolution in Paris in February 1848 brought the liberals and radicals together at a meeting in Heidelberg. There representatives from six states, including Prussia, discussed urgent changes in German political institutions on a national basis. Their decisions were published in the Declaration of Heidelberg:

1 Heidelberg, 5th March. Today fifty-one men were assembled here, from Prussia, Bavaria, Wurtemberg, Baden, Nassau and Frankfurt, almost all members of state assemblies, in order to discuss the most urgent measures for the Fatherland in this
5 moment of decision.

    Unanimously resolved in their devotion to the freedom, unity, independence and honour of the German nation, they all express their conviction that the establishment and defence of these highest blessings must be attempted by co-operation of all the German
10 peoples with their governments, so long as delivery is still possible in this manner.

    No less unanimous was the deep expression of sorrow that sad experience of the effectiveness of the German Confederation authorities has shaken confidence in them so much, that an address
15 of the citizens to them would evoke the worst discord.

    The assembled unanimously expressed their conviction of what the Fatherland urgently needs as follows:

    'Germany must not be involved in war through intervention in the affairs of the neighbouring country or through non-recognition
20 of the changes in the state made there.

    Germans must not be caused to diminish or rob from other nations the freedom and independence which they themselves ask as their right.

    The meeting of a national representation elected in all the Ger-
25 man lands according to the number of the people must not be postponed, both for the removal of imminent internal and external dangers, and for the development of the strength and flowering of German national life!'

At the same time they have agreed to concentrate their efforts so
30 that as soon as possible a more complete assembly of men of trust
from all German peoples should come together in order to continue
deliberation of this most important matter and to offer its co-
operation to the Fatherland as well as to the Governments.

To this end seven members were requested to prepare proposals
35 concerning the election and the establishment of an appropriate
national representation and speedily to take care of the invitations
to an assembly of German men.

A main task of the national representation will in any case be
common defence . . . and external representation, whereby great
40 sums of money will be saved for other important needs, while at the
same time the identity and suitable self-administration of the
different states remains in existence.

With the prudent, faithful and manly co-operation of all Germans, the Fatherland may hope to achieve and to maintain
45 freedom, unity and order in the most difficult situations, and
joyfully to greet the advent of a hardly expected strength and
flowering. . . .

* Invitations for the proposed 'assembly of German men' were quickly
issued, and the assembly met at the end of the month. This assembly is
known as the *Vorparlament*, usually translated as 'Pre-Parliament', but
better thought of as 'Preparatory Parliament', which was preparing the
way for the proposed national parliament, the real parliament.

The *Vorparlament* met at Frankfurt, chosen because it was already the
meeting place of the Diet of the Confederation. A total of 574 representatives, from almost all the states of the Confederation, squeezed themselves into the pews of the *Pauluskirche* (St. Paul's Church), where for the
next four days they talked and argued. Eventually they reached an
agreement on how to elect a national Constituent Assembly or Parliament. Once elected this Parliament was to draw up a constitution for a
united Germany.

It was decided that the Parliament should consist of one representative
for every 50 000 inhabitants and be elected by citizens, who were of age
and 'economically independent'. It was left to individual states to decide
who was an independent citizen. Some states decided on a residence
qualification, some on ownership of property. Although the *Vorparlament* did not actually say so, it was assumed that only men could vote, so
women were excluded from the franchise along with servants, farm
labourers and anyone receiving poor relief. This last category alone
excluded large numbers – in Cologne nearly a third of the population was
on poor relief.

a) *The Frankfurt Parliament*

In most states the elections were indirect. The voters elected 'electors', who in their turn chose representatives to be sent to the Assembly. The Assembly when it met in Frankfurt in May 1848 was therefore not very representative of the population as a whole. This was not surprising in view of the restrictions on those who could vote. Of the 596 members, the vast majority were middle class. There were large numbers of teachers, professors, lawyers and government officials. It was probably the best-educated Parliament ever – over 80 per cent of the members held university degrees, mostly in law. There were a few landowners, four craftsmen and one peasant.

Its composition made the Assembly, or Frankfurt Parliament as it came to be called, moderate liberal in politics. There was nothing radical, revolutionary or republican about it, apart from its small minority of extremist members. Its aim was to establish a united Germany under a constitutional monarch who would rule through an elected Parliament. It had been a great achievement to have got the Parliament elected, convened and ready to begin work in only a little over a month. Elections had been organized on a national scale for the first time and they had been carried out peacefully and successfully.

Now came the moment of truth. Could the Parliament carry out the programme which the *Vorparlament* had drawn up? Apart from drawing up a national constitution, which the *Vorparlament* saw as the main task of the Parliament, the programme recommended approval of a series of 'Basic Rights and Demands', such as freedom of the press, fair taxation, equality of political rights without regard to religion, separation of Church and State, and German citizenship for all.

The Parliament started by considering the relationship between itself and the individual states. The Confederation had been an association in which the state had a very large degree of independence from federal control. The authority of the Diet, never very impressive, had become weaker and more ineffective. The Frankfurt Parliament's intention was that the new 'Germany' should have much stronger central government, with correspondingly greater control over the actions of the states. It quickly decided that any national constitution which it framed would be sovereign, and that while state parliaments would be free to make state laws, they would only be valid if they did not conflict with that constitution. So by the end of May the Frankfurt Parliament had declared its authority over the states, their parliaments and Princes. Now it remained to draw up a constitution and to organize a government.

  * Most members of the Parliament could accept that the logical approach would be to agree a constitution and then to set up a government according to its terms. But it was another matter to find a majority of members who favoured any one procedure for carrying out these tasks, or who shared similar views on the details of the constitution established. Without the discipline imposed by well-organized political parties and without the dominance provided by outstanding leaders, the Frankfurt Parliament became a 'talking shop' in which it was very

difficult to reach agreement on anything.

It quickly became clear that it would not be possible to reach rapid agreement on a constitution. Steps were therefore taken to establish a provisional government to rule in the meantime. But although agreement was reached on generalities such as the powers of the provisional government, so little was agreed about the specific ways in which these powers were to be carried out that the 'Provisional Central Power' established at the end of June was largely ineffectual.

The Provisional Central Power provided for an Imperial Regent, or Vicar of the Empire, to be elected by the Parliament. He was to govern through ministers, appointed by him and responsible to Parliament, until such time as a decision about the constitution could be reached. An elderly Austrian Archduke, John, was elected as Regent. He was an unusual Archduke, married to the daughter of a village postmaster, and with known liberal views and German nationalist sympathies. He duly appointed a number of ministers but, as they did not have any staff or offices, and their duties were not clearly defined, they could do little.

As the summer went on, it seemed less and less likely that the German Confederation would be transformed into a united Germany by the efforts of the Parliament. Nevertheless, the Parliament did not give up, and continued its interminable debate over the constitution. In December, the Fifty Articles of the fundamental rights of the German citizen were approved and became law. For the Parliament to have reached this degree of agreement was by now an unexpected achievement. The Articles included equality before the law, freedom of worship and freedom of the press, freedom from arrest without warrant, and an end to discrimination because of class.

* Apart from the constitution, other problems beset the Parliament. One concerned the territorial extent of 'Germany'. Should it include all German-speaking lands, even those within that part of the Austrian Empire which lay outside the Confederation, or should it include only the states of the Confederation? The existing boundaries of the Confederation did not conform to any logical definition of 'Germany'. Parts of the Kingdom of Prussia and the Austrian Empire were included while others were not. Those parts that were within the Confederation contained many Czechs and Poles while some of the excluded provinces had an overwhelmingly German-speaking population. Seemingly most illogical of all, French-speaking Luxemburg, ruled over by the King of the Netherlands, was a part of the Confederation (see map on page 2).

So how, in this confusion, should the new German state be defined, bearing in mind the nationalist creed that a common language indicated a common racial origin? The Parliament was as usual divided between the members who wanted a *Grossdeutschland* (Great Germany) which would include the predominantly German-speaking provinces of the Austrian Empire, and those who favoured a *Kleindeutschland* (Little Germany) which would exclude Austria but include the whole of Prussia. The

Grossdeutschland plan would maintain the leadership of Germany by Catholic Austria, while the *Kleindeutschland* plan would leave Protestant Prussia as the dominant German state. The Parliament was unable to decide between the two proposals, and the argument dragged on inconclusively.

* Another problem worrying the Parliament involved the army. In order to exert its authority the central government would need a loyal army. The only army in any way capable of acting as a national army in 1848 was the Prussian one. A Prussian general was appointed as Minister of War, but he agreed to accept the post only on condition that the Prussian army would remain independent. In addition, he insisted that he could not act in any way contrary to the wishes of the King of Prussia. As Minister of War he did try to persuade the rulers of Bavaria and Austria, the only states which had armies of any significance, to join with Prussia if 'exceptional circumstances' should make it necessary to field a national German army, but he failed. Without an army loyal to it, the authority of the central power remained theory rather than fact.

* Throughout the winter of 1848–9 the Parliament continued its debate, and in March 1849, to many people's surprise, a Constitution for a German Empire was finally agreed. There were to be two houses, the lower house to be elected by a secret ballot among men over the age of 25 and of 'good reputation', the upper house to be made up of the reigning monarchs and princes of the Confederation. The two houses would have control over legislation and finance, and although the Emperor would have considerable power, he would only be able to hold up legislation for a limited time. A compromise between liberals and radicals was agreed, by which the radicals accepted the idea of a Prussian Emperor in return for concessions which made the franchise more democratic. The Parliament offered the Crown to the King of Prussia, but he refused it (see page 36). The rulers of Bavaria, Saxony and Hanover together with Prussia rejected the new constitution.

b) *The Failure of the Parliament*

In the face of these disappointments, many members of Parliament lost heart and Austrian and Prussian representatives went home. The remnants, about 130 of them, mostly from south German states, made one last attempt to recover the situation. They called for the election of the first new German Parliament, or *Reichstag*, in the following August, but the call fell on deaf ears. The moment was past, the high hopes gone. The Parliament was driven out of Frankfurt by the city government and moved to Stuttgart, the capital of the Kingdom of Württemberg. There it was forcibly dispersed by the King's soldiers in June 1849. So ended the Frankfurt experiment.

* Why did the Frankfurt Parliament fail? It started with the advantage that the old Diet of the Confederation had agreed to its own demise and

had nominated the Parliament as its legal successor. This meant the Parliament had no national rival. It was the sole national representative body. But this was its only advantage, and its only strength. Its disadvantages and weaknesses were many and decisive.

There were two main reasons for the Parliament's failure. One was the divisions among its members, which so slowed down the making of decisions that it missed the opportunity of filling the power vacuum that existed in much of Germany in the second half of 1848. The radical minority, who wanted to change society, do away with the princes and replace them with a republic, were less concerned with constitution making than with the overthrow of existing governments. They found themselves in conflict with the majority of liberal members who wanted a moderate settlement which would safeguard both the rights of individual states and of the central government, and with a minimum of social change. A written constitution accepted by the national monarch would protect the rights of an elected parliament within a reorganized Confederation. There was also a small conservative group who wanted to preserve the rights of individual states and ensure that neither the Frankfurt Parliament nor the central government would exercise too much control. These groups were not organized like modern political parties, but were loose undisciplined associations within which there were many shades of opinion and divergent belief. In addition to the three main groups there were a large number of independent, politically uncommitted members. For much of the time it proved impossible to resolve the differences between the members sufficently to arrive at even a majority decision. This was something that the liberals, because of their numerical superiority, had not expected, and with which they were unable to deal successfully. This wide and unresolved division of opinion within the Parliament doomed it to failure almost from the start because it was unable to take the decisive action without which there could be no hope of success.

The Parliament was further handicapped by its unwise choice of leader, Heinrich von Gagern. He was a distinguished liberal politician, sincere and well meaning, but without the force of character needed to dominate the assembly and direct the debate.

The other main reason for failure was the fact that the authority of Parliament had never been accepted wholeheartedly by the individual states. Also, the Parliament lacked effective administration. No proper government organization was set up, and there was no military backing to enforce its decrees. Without these, the decisions it took were unlikely to be implemented. In many ways it was a triumph for the Frankfurt Parliament ever to have met, given the difficulties of arranging elections at short notice in 39 states. That it failed to achieve its aims was predictable, given the inexperience of its members and the opposition of the rulers who generally wished to restore the status quo.

When the ruling monarchs and princes feared that they were about to lose many of their powers or even their thrones because of revolutions within their own territories, they were generally prepared to appear to support the work of the Frankfurt Parliament in case, by opposing it, they should stir up more opposition to their rule. But once the rulers were able to re-establish their authority they lost all reason to support the parliamentarians who seemed certain to attempt to diminish the powers of the individual states in favour of the larger states, especially Austria and Prussia. When the new Austrian Emperor, Franz Joseph, regained control of all his territories in March 1849, all hope of a *Grossdeutschland* disappeared. It was well known that the Austrian government would have nothing to do with such a revolutionary change. And once effective Austrian opposition was established, it was almost certain that no other ruler would dare to be seen to be taking the lead in establishing a German Empire, even if he had supported the establishment of a liberal Empire of the type the parliamentarians envisaged. Thus the Frankfurt Parliament, which had at first seemed to offer the way forward for national revival, became an irrelevancy and embarrassment whose continued existence offered the possibility of further social and political upheavals. Most rulers were pleased to see it go.

3 Prussia

In the immediate future the hopes of the German nationalists lay with Prussia, and her King Frederick William IV. Frederick William was a strange and complex character, sensitive, artistic, cultured and charming, but moody and unpredictable and so unstable that later in life he was to be declared insane. He was obsessed by a romantic and highly inaccurate vision of the Middle Ages, and looked back nostalgically to the days of the Holy Roman Empire and an unquestioned belief in the divine right of Kings. He had a mystical idea of kingship and its privileges and duties.

1 I am moved to declare solemnly that no power on earth will ever
   succeed in prevailing on me to transform the natural relationship
   between prince and people . . . into a constitutional one. Never
   will I permit a written sheet of paper to come between our God in
5 Heaven and this land . . . to rule us with its paragraphs and
   supplement the old sacred loyalty.

At the beginning of his reign in 1840 it seemed that Frederick William might be a reforming monarch, who would make the government more liberal and democratic. He released political prisoners, abolished censorship and gave greater power to the eight provincial Diets in Prussia, but these concessions had the opposite effect to that which he expected. Instead of calming unrest, they increased it. They encouraged liberal agitation for a proper constitution as promised in the Vienna Settlement of 1815 and they upset the conservative-minded *Junker* nobility. Angered by opposition, Frederick William returned to restrictive policies. He suppressed newspapers criticizing his government, particularly articles by Karl Marx. Then in 1847 he swung back to what at first seemed more liberal ideas and called a meeting of the United Diet in Berlin (see page 15). This uncertain wavering between the traditional conservative autocrat and the liberal monarch was a facet of his general instability and was a pattern which Frederick William was to repeat many times during the revolutions of 1848 and the events of 1849.

   * When the news of the revolution in Paris reached Berlin, a demonstration by workers, mostly self-employed craftsmen, took place in the palace square on 13 March 1848. The demonstrators threw stones at the troops and the troops replied by opening fire with cannon and rifles. 'Ferocious scenes' followed. Deputations of leading citizens called on the King and asked him to make political concessions, while fighting continued in a confused way during the next two days. The craftsmen were joined by factory workers and others. The original demonstrations began as a protest about pay and working conditions, but quickly turned into a general, if vague, demand for 'the maintenance of the rights irrefutably belonging to the people of the state'.

   Three days later, on 16 March, news of revolution in Vienna and the dismissal of Metternich reached Berlin, and popular excitement rose even further. A large crowd collected outside the royal palace. The King appeared on the balcony and was loudly cheered. He then ordered the troops to clear the crowds, and shots were fired either in panic or by accident after some jostling and grabbing at horses' reins had taken place. The crowd shouted 'Down with the army' and a riot broke out. Fighting was fierce.

1   Everywhere students, citizens, artisans and working men rushed
    into the streets, supplied themselves with weapons, ammunition,
    axes and iron bars and rushed to the barricades, which in some
    streets reached to the first floor windows. By seven o'clock most of
5   the Königstrasse had been taken by the soldiers – the whole street
    swam with blood.

   Fighting continued during the night, and at least three hundred rioters were killed, and large numbers injured or arrested.

   The King, who all his life hated bloodshed and, most untypically for a Prussian, disliked the army and all military matters, decided to make a personal appeal for peace and calm. He wrote a letter 'To my dear Berliners' at 3 a.m. Copies were quickly printed and were put up on trees in the city centre early on the morning of Sunday, 19 March. It promised that the troops would be withdrawn if the street barricades were demolished. The concluding sentence read:

1   Listen to the paternal voice of your King, you inhabitants of my
    true and beautiful Berlin; and forget the past, as I shall forget it, for

the sake of that great future, which under the peace-giving blessing of God, is dawning upon Prussia, and through Prussia upon all
5 Germany.

For a time it seemed that the impossible might happen, absolutism might give way to democracy and Frederick William might become a popular, constitutional monarch.

1   In the course of the morning of 21st the King appeared in the streets
     on horseback with the German colours, black, red and gold, round
     his arm. He was greeted with tumultuous applause . . . he stopped
     and said 'I am truly proud that it is my capital, where so
5   powerful an opinion has manifested itself. This day is a great day
     and ought never to be forgotten. The colours I wear are not my own;
     I do not mean to usurp anything with them. . . . I want liberty; I
     will have unity in Germany'. He spoke again of German unity in a
     proclamation issued on the same day 'From this day forth
10   the name of Prussia is fused and dissolved in that of Germany'.

What were Frederick William's motives for this behaviour? It is sometimes argued that by riding through the streets wearing the black, red and gold 'colours of freedom' he was not submitting to the revolution from necessity, nor joining it out of conviction, but by putting himself at its head was trying to take it over and so regain control. The argument can be taken further. The reference in his later proclamation to Prussia being absorbed in Germany has been interpreted as an attempt by Frederick William to overcome the dangers of the Prussian revolution by proposing himself as the leader of a German national revolution. It seems more probable, in view of his unstable character, that he was carried away by the emotion of the occasion and felt, at least for a short time, that he was indeed destined to be a popular monarch and national leader.

* In the following days Frederick William granted a series of general reforms, accepted constitutional government in principle and agreed to the election of an assembly to draw up a new constitution for Prussia. He appeared the very model of a liberal monarch. But his change of heart did not last long. As soon as he had escaped from Berlin, he expressed very different feelings. He spoke of humiliation at the way he had been forced to make concessions to the people, no longer his 'dear Berliners', and made it clear that he now believed there could be no close relationship between a king and his subjects.

Nevertheless, he kept his word. Elections were held for the new assembly as promised and liberal ministers were appointed. The assembly began to debate a new constitution for Prussia, but before its work was completed Frederick William dissolved the assembly and proclaimed a constitution of his own.

* The Prussian constitution of late 1848 was a strange mixture of liberal policies and absolutism. There was to be a representative

assembly, with two houses. The upper house would be elected by older property owners, and the lower one by manhood suffrage. The King could, however, in emergency suspend civil rights and collect taxes without reference to Parliament. Ministers were to be appointed and dismissed by the King, and were to be responsible only to him and not to Parliament. The King would also have the right to alter the written constitution at anytime it suited him to do so.

The new proposals were well received in Prussia, and ministers made no secret of the fact that they hoped it would be a better model for a united Germany than the Frankfurt Parliament. They had amibitions to make Prussia the leading state in Germany, and Frederick William the leading monarch. They hoped that Germany would be united not by a national Parliament, but by control imposed by Prussia.

* In March 1849 the Frankfurt Parliament voted, halfheartedly (290 votes in favour, 240 abstentions), to elect Frederick William as Emperor of a united Germany. A deputation set off to offer him the crown, but he refused it:

1 About the crown which the *Pauluskirche* has for sale; every German
   nobleman is a hundred times too good to accept such a diadem
   moulded out of the dirt and dregs of revolution, disloyalty and
   treason . . . if accepted, it demands from me incalculable sacrifices
5 and burdens me with heavy duties. The German National
   Assembly has counted on me in all things, which were calculated to
   establish the unity, power and glory of Germany. I feel honoured by
   their confidence . . . but I should not justify that confidence if I,
   violating sacred rights, were, without the voluntary assent of the
10 crowned princes and free states of our Fatherland, to take a resolu-
   tion, which must be of decisive importance to them and to the states
   which they rule'.

Frederick William declined the crown on the grounds that it was not the Parliament's to offer. He would only accept it if the offer came from his equals, his fellow princes. He distrusted 'the gentlemen of Frankfurt' who had, he believed, taken it upon themselves to speak for a united Germany without any legal authority. In any case he was not prepared to be Emperor of Germany if it meant putting himself and the Kingdom of Prussia under the control of the Frankfurt Parliament. It is ironic that Frederick William, who all his life, dreamed of reviving the glories of the Holy Roman Empire, felt unable to accept the Imperial crown of a new German Empire when it was offered to him.

4 Failure of the Revolutions

By 1850 it seemed as if the events of the two previous years had never been; nothing had changed in most of the states. All traces of the Frankfurt Parliament were quickly cleared away. The black, red and gold 'flag of freedom' was removed from the hall of the Diet. The ships which the Parliament had bought as the nucleus of a national fleet were sold off at auction.

Constitutional changes obtained from their rulers in Saxony, Hanover and several smaller states were revoked, and liberals all over Germany were arrested and imprisoned. Some were even executed. The lucky ones escaped into exile. In Prussia police powers were increased and local government powers reduced. The 'three-class suffrage' was introduced in elections for the Prussian lower house. This system, based on tax liability, ensured that the richest sectors of society would be the most fully represented.

* Why was so little achieved in Germany in the revolutions of 1848-9? Active revolution was comparatively slight. In Prussia it was restricted to riots in Berlin and unrest in the Rhineland and Silesia. In the small states of the south-west, poverty stricken peasants attacked their landlords, castles were stormed and property destroyed. In Baden a people's republic was briefly proclaimed. It had little support and was quickly suppressed by the liberal government. Most revolutionary activity in Germany did not involve armed uprisings. Meetings, peaceful demonstrations and petitions were the chief weapons of the revolution. There was little fighting.

The years leading up to 1848 had seen increased political activity. In 1846 the Grand Duke of Baden had been forced to accept a liberal constitution, and the following year the Elector of Hesse-Cassel had been prevented from making reactionary changes to the local constitution. In 1848 other rulers gave in easily, if temporarily, to demands for more democratic governments. They seem generally to have felt that to oppose the widespread demands for political change might lead to their overthrow. The sensible course of action was to give way on easily reversed issues until the discontent subsided. But in those states where the rulers granted concessions, willing or unwillingly, they wisely retained control of their armed forces. All they had to do was simply wait for an opportunity to regain power. Growing disunity among the revolutionaries gave them that opportunity. There were wide differences in the political aims of liberals and radicals. While the former wanted constitutional government in all states and a united Empire with a national parliament, the latter worked for complete social and political change within a republican framework. Nor were the nationalists united in their specifications. There was no agreement on the form the new Germany should take – a unified state or a federation, a monarchy or republic, *Grossdeutschland* or *Kleindeutschland*?

Class differences added to the disunity. The majority of workers and peasants had a purely practical and immediate revolutionary aim: the removal of the intolerable pressures on their lives. They were not concerned with political ideologies, but their radical leaders were. Because most liberals were middle class the radical-liberal conflict merged into a wider class struggle.

Popular enthusiasms are often short lived and within a few months much of the active support for national unity and a national parliament had disappeared. This loss of support was encouraged by the slow progress being made by the Frankfurt Parliament.

All these divisive elements weakened the revolutions, but in the end they failed because the enemy was stronger, better organized and above all possessed military power. The story might have been very different in Berlin if there had not been a well equipped, well trained army available to the King and his government. Given their military and economic advantages, their determination and often their ruthlessness, the Princes were bound to win in the end. Constitutional government and national unity could only be achieved on their terms, not through the well intentioned but ineffectual efforts of a liberal parliament, or by the unco-ordinated actions of popular revolt. And it was clear in 1848 that attractive as might be the idea of a strong and united Germany in theoretical terms, the rulers felt that they had too much to lose by supporting the practicalities of unification offered by the Frankfurt Parliament. Generally they had no wish to see their powers limited by liberal constitutions and a powerful central authority. In any case, once order was restored in the Austrian Empire and the policy from Vienna was still based on dominating Germany by keeping her weak and divided, there was no possibility of any moves towards a more united Germany being allowed to take place. Germany would only be unified once the military might and moral authority of the Austrian Empire had been overcome.

Making Notes on 'Germany in Revolution 1848–49'

Your notes on this chapter should give you an understanding of the causes of the revolutionary movements of 1848–9 and of the political and constitutional developments associated with them. You should also have a framework on which to base a discussion of the reason why, in the end, so little was achieved. In addition you should have an outline of the important events taking place in Prussia in the same year.

The following headings and subheadings should be helpful in making your notes:

1.   Causes of Revolutionary Movements
1.1. Population changes
1.2. Economic problems
           in the countryside
           in the town
1.3. Popular demands
1.4. Middle class
1.5. Political movements

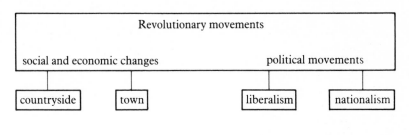

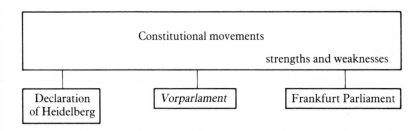

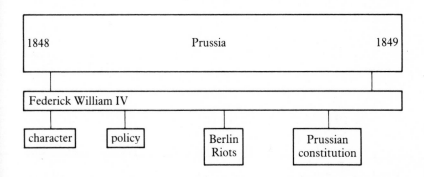

Summary – Germany in revolution, 1848–49

2.   Constitutional Movements
2.1. Baden
2.2. Declaration of Heidelberg
2.3. The *Vorparlament*
2.4. The Frankfurt Parliament

Answering essay questions on '*Germany in Revolution 1848–49*'

You may need to use the information from this chapter to answer general questions of the type discussed on page 105, but you are quite likely to be asked questions concentrating just on the events of these two very important years.

An example of such a question is:

> Why did the Frankfurt Parliament fail to achieve its aims? (Cambridge, 1981)

This is a straightforward 'Why' question. Construct an essay plan by going through the following three stages:

1. Make a list of statements which provide a direct answer to this question. Begin each with the word 'because' for example 'because it was unrepresentative' and 'because it lacked effective power'. There should be six or seven statements.

2. List the facts you need to include for each statement to substantiate it.

3. Decide on an order of importance for your statements. Number them accordingly. Would you start with the most or the least important? Why?

Another question on this period, for which it would also be well worth making an essay plan, is:

> Why did the revolutionaries of 1848 achieve so little in Germany? (WJEC, 1982)

What would you include in an answer to this question that you have not included in the essay plan for the first question?

Source-based questions on, 'Germany in Revolution 1848–49'

1   German nationalism, 1847

Read carefully the extract from Prince Hohenlohe's Memorandum, given on page 26. Answer the following questions:
a) In one sentence describe the main idea of his argument.
b) Hohenlohe makes several assertions presented as fact, not as opinion. Identify two such assertions and comment on their validity.
c) Does Hohenlohe rely more on reason or on emotion to persuade his readers of the rightness of his argument? Explain your answer.

2   The Declaration of Heidelberg, 1848

Read carefully the extracts from the Declaration of Heidelberg, given on page 27. Answer the following questions:
a) What policies did the authors favour in foreign affairs?
b) What was the attitude of the Declaration's authors towards the existing governments of the German states? Explain your answer.
c) What evidence do the extracts contain to suggest that the 51 men who met at Heidelberg were generally conservative in economic and social matters?

3   Civil disturbances, 1848

Read carefully the description of the riot in Berlin, given on page 34, and answer the following questions:
a) Who, according to the author of the extract, took part in the fighting against the soldiers? What tentative conclusions could you reach from a detailed consideration of the words he uses to describe the rioters?
b) What internal evidence does the extract contain to suggest that this account is unlikely to be reliable in matters of factual detail?

4   The views of Frederick William IV

Read carefully the four extracts from the writings and reported speeches of Frederick William IV, given on pages 33, 34, 35 and 36. Answer the following questions:
a) Describe Frederick William's attitude towards the Divine Right of Kings, using evidence from the extract on page 33.
b) Does the concluding sentence of Frederick William's letter 'To my dear Berliners', quoted on page 34, support or contradict the attitude shown in the extract on page 33? Explain your answer.
c) What reasonable explanations could be offered for Frederick William's actions as described in the extract on page 35?
d) What reasons does Frederick William give for not accepting the offer of the Imperial crown from the Frankfurt Parliament?
e) What suggestions can be made about the attitudes and character of Frederick William IV using evidence from the four extracts?

CHAPTER 3

Prussia and Austria 1849–66

1 Austrian Ascendancy

Historians are fond of describing the 1850s as a low point in the history of Prussia. At this time Prussia had an international reputation for weakness and was regarded very much as the least important of the major Powers. But appearances were deceptive, for the foundations were being laid for the unification of Germany under Bismarck.

Despite the failure of the Frankfurt Parliament and Frederick William's refusal to accept the imperial crown, there were still, in 1849, supporters of German nationalism in Prussia. One of these was General von Radowitz, an old friend of Frederick William. He had been a right-wing representative of Prussia in the Frankfurt Parliament. Despite his conservative beliefs, he also supported social reform and a closer relationship between crown and people. He was an ardent nationalist and an equally ardent monarchist, and devoted himself for the next two years to working on plans for a united Germany under Prussian leadership, which would be acceptable to Frederick William.

In 1849 Radowitz proposed a scheme which met with Frederick William's approval. The 'Prussian Union Plan' for a united *Kleindeutschland* suggested a German Federal *Reich* (Empire), which would exclude Austria. It would have a strong central government and would give the King of Prussia control of the federal army. Although Austria would not be a member of the *Reich*, there would be a special relationship, a permanent 'union', between the *Reich* and the Habsburg Empire. This union would form a *Grossdeutschland* in which Austria and Prussia would be equal, but there would be no central government no any parliamentary assembly. The *Reich* itself would be based on the constitution drawn up by the Frankfurt Parliament, with Prussia as the leading state and the King of Prussia as Emperor. This complicated plan, which tried to provide both *Kleindeutschland* and *Grossdeutschland* solutions, was not acceptable to Austria. The chief minister, Schwarzenberg, saw it as a devious scheme to reduce Austrian influence in Germany. He was not, however, immediately able to mount effective opposition to it, as internal Austrian problems were occupying his attention. This allowed Prussia to press on with the plan. A 'Three King's Alliance' between Prussia, Saxony and Hanover was the first step. Then a number of smaller states were persuaded to fall in with the Prussian proposals. Encouraged by his success, Radowitz called a meeting of representatives of all the German states to Erfurt to inaugurate the new *Reich*. But the response was poor. Only Prussia and a few small states attended the meeting, for the majority of states were both suspicious of Prussian ambitions and fearful of Austria's reaction.

Schwarzenberg, having overcome his revolutionary difficulties in Austria, was now free to move on to the offensive. He put forward a scheme of his own for a *Grossdeutschland* to be governed jointly by delegates from Austria, Prussia and the larger German states. Attracted by the way in which this proposal seemed to offer them greater political influence, some of the larger states such as Hanover and Saxony deserted Prussia and gave their support to Austria. Schwarzenberg was now able to summon the Diet of the old German Confederation, thought to have been dead and buried, to meet in Frankfurt in May 1850. The response was good and he was able to announce that the corpse had been revived and that the Diet and the Confederation were both alive and well.

   * Who spoke for Germany – Prussia and the Erfurt Parliament, or Austria and the Frankfurt Diet? The two Powers were about to begin their struggle for control of Germany. It began in the small state of Hesse-Cassel and for a time it looked as if full-scale war would break out.

The Elector of Hesse-Cassel (the state's ruler) had quarrelled with the parliament and appealed to the Austrian controlled Diet at Frankfurt for help. But the Prussian controlled Parliament at Erfurt claimed the right to decide the dispute. Hesse-Cassel was of strategic importance to Prussia because it separated the main part of Prussia from the Prussian Rhineland, and therefore controlled communications between the two.

The Prussian army mobilized, and Austria replied with an ultimatum that only the troops of the old Confederation had the right to intervene. Small-scale fighting broke out between Prussian and Austrian troops, but Manteuffel, the new Prussian Minister-President (Prime Minister), and his Minister of War had very little faith in their army. They were anxious to avoid all-out war.

   * A meeting between Manteuffel and Schwarzenberg was arranged at Olmütz and on 29 November, 1850 Prussia agreed both to abandon the Prussian Union Plan as it was clear that it was only supported by a minority of German states and to a conference of states being held at Dresden early in 1851 to discuss the future of Germany. The Schwarzenberg plan for a *Grossdeutschland*, which he had put forward as an alternative to the Prussian Union Plan, was not acceptable to the smaller German states, as it would have increased the power of the larger states at their expense. There was strong pressure for a return to the status quo of before the 1848 revolution and Prussia supported this at the Conference. The Prussian Union Plan was lost, and anything was better than accepting the Austrian counterplan. In May 1851 the German Confederation of 1815 was formally re-established and an alliance between Austria and Prussia appeared to signal a return to the policy of close co-operation. Everything was as it had been; all signs of the events of the previous three years had been carefully covered over and consigned to decent obscurity.

   * Politically, Prussia was deeply humiliated by what in effect was a surrender to Austria and the destruction of all hopes of Prussian

domination of a united Germany. Economically, however, the story was very different. Manteuffel encouraged the development of trade and industry. Financial help was given to depressed industries and courts were set up to settle industrial disputes. In the 1850s industrial production and foreign trade doubled. Prices rose, but so did the standard of living. The Prussian government worked through the *Zollverein* towards an extension of the free trade area. Most industries benefited and the Prussian economy expanded. In the struggle for the control of Germany, Prussia might have been too weak to tackle Austria on the battlefield, but economically her power, and therefore her ability to finance a full-scale war in the future, was increasing rapidly year by year.

Smaller German states needed trade with Prussia. They could not afford to stay outside the *Zollverein*, for the economic advantages of alliance with protectionist Austria were not nearly as attractive as those to be had by joining with the free trade *Zollverein*. To combat this, the Austrian government proposed an extended customs union to include Austria and those German states still outside the *Zollverein* which would have a moderate protectionist policy. The intentions were political rather than economic. Schwarzenberg had written to the Austrian Emperor in 1851 saying that the best way for Austria to achieve supremacy in Germany was by taking a lead in promoting economic unity. The Austrian plan failed because of lack of support among the German states. Bavaria, Hanover, Württemberg and Hesse refused to join the proposed Austrio–German customs union; they preferred to side with Prussia, and the economically successful *Zollverein*. Schwarzenberg's plan collapsed, leaving Prussia in economic control of Germany.

* Schwarzenberg died in 1852, and in the next few years Austria became militarily involved with problems in south eastern Europe. In order to be free to deal with these, Austria signed a treaty with Prussia, agreeing to maintain the status quo in Germany for the time being and agreeing not to interfere in German affairs. Despite the development of railways, considerable industrial expansion and rapidly rising exports, the Austrian economy was in difficulties. Taxation was not sufficient to finance the newly reformed central administration, which became corrupt, nor to maintain the army, which became more and more inefficient.

In Prussia the economy was booming. Capital was freely available as the result of increased foreign trade. Mining of coal and iron continued to develop rapidly to provide the basis of an industrial economy. A stock exchange was opened in Berlin to encourage and regulate investment in industry. The railways were flourishing and the length of line was doubled during the 1850s. At the end of the Crimean war in 1856, Prussia was economically stable and industrially expanding; Austria was economically and financially vulnerable, crippled by the cost of keeping her large armies mobilized during the war, and in no state to cope with the depression which swept across Europe in the late 1850s.

Prussia, by remaining strictly neutral during the war, benefited politically as well as economically, and managed to keep on good terms with the other European Powers especially Russia. Austria also remained neutral, but in name only, and gained little respect as the result of her wavering diplomacy, sometimes siding against Russia, sometimes against Britain and France. By 1856 she had lost the friendship of Russsia without obtaining that of Britain and France. At one point in the war Austria had attempted to mobilize the forces of the German Confederation against Russia, but had been thwarted in the Diet at Frankfurt by a Prussian representative, Otto von Bismarck.

2 Prussia 1850–62

During the 1850s in Prussia, Manteuffel showed himself to be a conservative reformer. He was prepared to accept limited change as long as it did not lead to any extension of parliamentary influence. He had a particular hatred of the liberal, educated, professional class, considering them to be arrogant, cowardly and godless. He believed the best way to stabilize society and reduce the chance of revolution was to improve the living conditions of peasants and workers.

He was especially concerned to help the peasants, because he believed that they were the basis of popular support for the monarchy. He persuaded Frederick William IV to free all the peasants from their traditional feudal obligations to their landlords. Special low interest government loans were available to enable peasants to buy their land, and 600 000 did so. In some parts of Prussia, where peasants had moved away to the towns looking for work, there was underpopulation in the countryside, but elsewhere there was overpopulation and great pressure on land. Where this was the case the government encouraged emigration, and gave peasants financial help to move to less populated areas of the country.

In towns the government set out to help factory workers. Payment of a standard minimum wage was strongly encouraged. Employers were no longer allowed to pay wages in overpriced goods instead of money. Financial help was given to industry, inspectors were appointed to improve working conditions in factories, and children under 12 were forbidden to do factory work.

In these ways Manteuffel aimed to unite the monarchy with its most underprivileged subjects. He believed that ministers had a duty to govern well, and that this meant governing in the best interests of all the people. If the ordinary people were happy and contented, the monarchy would not be undermined by liberals and socialists using social discontent to stir up trouble and possible revolution. At the same time he believed that ministers had a right to govern without reference to the people, and that there was therefore no need for representative assemblies of any kind. He governed without Parliament for the whole of his

time as Minister-President (1850–1858). In other ways he was equally reactionary, imposing strict censorship of the press and restrictions on the freedom of political parties to hold meetings. Prussia in the 1850s was thus a curious mixture, politically reactionary and repressive, socially reforming and economically prosperous.

* Frederick William, whose mental balance had always been precarious, became more and more unstable, until, in 1858, he was finally declared insane. His brother William became regent, and when Frederick William died in 1861, he succeeded to the throne as William I of Prussia. William, in complete contrast to Frederick William, was a typical Prussian soldier, practical, hardheaded and inflexible. Only Bismarck, his Chief Minister for nearly the whole of his reign, was ever able to make him change his mind. William was already 63 when he became king, but he was to reign for another 27 years. A devout Protestant, he believed that he was answerable only to God, which made it difficult to argue with him. He was prepared to listen to advice from ministers, but not necessarily to act on it. At heart he was an absolutist.

As a soldier the strengthening of the army was one of William's main concerns. He believed it was the key to the future greatness of Prussia. The war in Italy in 1859 between France and Austria showed up some alarming deficiencies in the Prussian army. Popular feeling in Germany favoured support for Austria and despite the rivalry between Prussia and Austria, Willam offered help. In return he demanded Austria should accept that Prussia was the leading German state. To make sure that the Austrians understood, he mobilized part of the Prussian army. The mobilization was a disaster. The army was in a state of confusion and quite unready to fight. Before it could be organized into some degree of order and readiness, the Austrians had been defeated in Italy and had made peace with France. The delay had lost William the opportunity to complete his bargain with Austria.

* As a result of this ignominious failure, William appointed a new Minister of War, General von Roon, and the following year a Bill to reform and modernize the Army was introduced into the Prussian Parliament. It provided for three instead of two years compulsory military service, an increase in the size of the army and a reform of its organization. To re-equip the army with new weapons, and to raise 49 new regiments would be expensive. The military budget would have to be greatly increased.

In the 1858 elections the liberals had won a large majority in Parliament, and they were opposed to the expenditure of so much money on the army. They believed there was always a danger that the government might use the army, not for the defence of Prussia from foreign attack, but against its own people as had happened in 1848. The liberals were particularly upset by the proposals to make the *Landwehr* (a semi-civilian, middle-class reserve force) into a part of the regular army. They would only agree to approve the increased military budget for one year and would not agree to extend the term of military service from two years to three. It was the beginning of a feud between William and the liberals about the army, which was to last for the rest of his reign. More than that, it was the beginning of a constitutional crisis over the balance of power between King and Parliament, which was also to last for many years.

William wanted 'his' army to be disciplined and loyal, a support for the monarch in time of danger at home and a defence for the state in time of danger abroad. In 1862, however, he needed a chief minister who could push the army reforms through Parliament, even against the wishes of the liberal majority. The choice fell on Otto von Bismarck.

3 Bismarck

Otto von Bismarck was born in 1815, the year of Waterloo. His father was a *Junker*, 'moderately wealthy and rather stupid'. The *Junkers* were the landowning nobility, with their own rules of conduct based on an elaborate code of honour, a strong devotion to the military life which was one of the few careers open to a true *Junker*, a strong sense of service to the Prussian state and an even stronger sense of their own importance. They were on the whole solid, unimaginative, conservative, bigoted and dull. Bismarck was proud of his *Junker* descent and all his life liked to present himself as a *Junker* squire, sometimes playing the part in a rather exaggerated way. He was often described as a 'typical *Junker*', which he was not. He was too clever and too enterprising for that.

Bismarck's mother came from a middle-class family of Hamburg merchants. Many of her relatives were civil servants, university professors or lawyers. All were educated, intelligent and articulate, and politically liberal. Bismarck seems to have been ashamed of this side of his family, and spoke of them in a disparaging way, comparing them unfavourably with his *Junker* ancestors. He did not get on well with his mother, who was so much livelier and cleverer than his father, but from her he inherited his intelligence, his quick wittedness and his determination.

At her insistence, he was sent away to school in Berlin, where he proved resistant to education, although he later became a good linguist, fluent in French, English and Russian. He was an excellent sportsman, being a good swimmer and rider, a crack shot and an expert fencer. He went on to university, where he wasted a good deal of time and money, drank too much and got into debt. A description of Bismarck at this time portrays him

1   . . . strutting down the street, wearing the usual beer-cap of
     crimson and gold, a dressing gown, enormously wide trousers and
     boots with iron spurs and heels. He carried an oak cudgel and wore
     a leather belt round his waist supporting two large pistols and a
5   heavy duelling sword.

A long scar across his face was the result of a recent duel, the only occasion in his year at Göttingen University when he was wounded in the 25 duels which he fought, and only then because his opponent's sword broke. At the end of a year he transferred to the University of Berlin, where he managed to pass his law examinations.

Success in these examinations was the entry to the Prussian Civil Service and Bismarck spent the next four years as a less than committed civil servant, eventually leaving his job, because he 'could not put up with superiors'. A reluctant year of military service followed, enjoyed neither by Bismarck nor the army. On his mother's death in 1839, he retired to help run the family estates. Country life soon bored him, and he found entertainment chasing after peasant girls and playing wild practical jokes on his neighbours, so that he became known as 'the mad *Junker*'.

He was a large man who ate and drank to excess. He smoked 14 cigars a day, and said he hoped to smoke 10 000 before his death, as well as drink 5000 bottles of champagne, not to mention untold quantities of brandy and beer. He ate huge meals, and not surprisingly suffered from chronic indigestion for many years. In 1883 when his weight reached 114 kilos, he was put on a diet of herrings and eventually managed to lose 25 kilos.

* Despite his solid appearance, Bismarck was very emotional and easily moved to tears or anger. His relations with William I were stormy; their meetings often degenerated into slanging matches, and Bismarck once pulled the handle off the door as he left the room, so great were his feelings of tension. His temper was violent, particularly when faced with strong opposition. He was ruthless, determined and unscrupulous in getting his own way, but he could also be charming and witty, a delightful companion and entertaining conversationalist.

He always had an eye for women, and was involved in a number of scandals and passionate love affairs. One of these, with the daughter of an English clergyman, led to him following her and her family all over Europe. When she married someone else, Bismarck sought consolation in a frenetic and disastrous bout of gambling, which all his life was one of his main recreations. A complex character, he was far from being the conventional *Junker* he liked people to think him.

By the time he was thirty, in 1845, Bismarck had achieved little. His energies and abilities were being wasted. He was becoming bored and lazy, without purpose, when in 1847 two events occurred which changed the direction of his life. He married Johanna von Puttkamer, a deeply religious Lutheran. 'I like piety in women and have a horror of female cleverness', he wrote. Johanna satisfied both his requirements in a wife, for she was pious, but was not clever. She did, however, provide a stable background for Bismarck, brought up their numerous children and overlooked his continued infidelities. When he fell in love with the wife of the Russian Ambassador, Johanna wrote, 'My soul has no room for jealousy and I rejoice greatly that my husband has found this charming woman'. Afterwards, as always, Johanna welcomed him back. She and the children remained an important part of his life, despite his later quarrels with his eldest son. As an old man he remarked that the fact that God had not taken any of his children was what gave him greatest happiness in his life.

a) *Political beginnings*

The other event of 1847 was Bismarck's election to the Prussian United Diet. It marked his entry into public life, but at the time no one, and certainly not Bismarck himself, could have forseen the political career which lay ahead of him in the next 43 years.

During the March days of the Berlin riots in 1848, Bismarck involved himself in counter-revolutionary plots. He was a member of the right-wing *Junker* Party and excessively anti-liberal 'Only two things matter for Prussia', he said, 'to avoid an alliance with democracy and to secure equality with Austria.'

* Bismarck implies in his memoirs that from the start of his political career he was working for the unification of Germany, that he planned to reform the army, make war on Austria and destroy the Confederation. Some historians believe that Bismarck did have a long-term plan, while others, such as A. J. P. Taylor, argue that he followed a day-to-day policy acting as seemed expedient. What evidence is there about Bismarck's political ideas in the years before 1862?

In newspapers articles in 1850 Bismarck demanded equality with Austria in the Confederation, and in December of that year he spoke in the Erfurt Parliament in defence of Frederick William's 'surrender' to Austria at Olmütz. He argued that a state should fight only in its own interest – what he called 'state egoism' – and war for Hesse-Cassel would have been foolish.

1 Gentlemen, show me an objective worth a war and I will go along with you . . . woe to any statesman who fails to find a cause of war which will stand up to scrutiny once the fighting is over.

This speech gained promotion for Bismarck in 1850 as Prussian envoy to the revived Diet of the Confederation at Frankfurt, where, apart from a short time in Vienna as Prussian ambassador, he remained until 1859. During his years at Frankfurt he gained an unenviable reputation for aggressive bad manners. He became increasingly anti-Austrian and was more and more convinced that war between Prussia and Austria was unavoidable. He argued that such a conflict would eventually lead to a divided Germany with a Protestant north and a Catholic south.

By 1856 as a result of the Crimean War Austria's prestige was reduced. She presented less of a threat in Bismarck's reckoning and he began referring to war not just as probable but as inevitable. He proposed negotiations with Russia and France as possible allies in any such future war. By 1858 he was arguing that Prussia should seek support among

Bismarck in 1858 (painting)

Bismarck in 1858 (photograph)

German nationalists and a year later that Austria should be driven out of the Confederation and a *Kleindeutschland* established under Prussian control. This was a theme he continued to develop over the next two years.

By the early 1860s he had a reputation as a tough, able politician, ambitious and ruthless. His defence of Frederick William's policy in his speech after Olmütz had established him as a loyal supporter of the monarchy, and he was known to favour an absolutist government, at least in a moderate form, and to have little time for parliamentary niceties.

b) *Minister-President*

William I was at loggerheads with his Parliament over the Army Bill and was threatening to abdicate unless Parliament gave in. The Minister of War, von Roon, sent a coded telegram to Bismarck in Paris, where he was now Prussian ambassador, summoning him to Berlin. William did not like what he knew of Bismarck, but was persuaded to see him. Bismarck described the meeting:

1 The situation only became clear to me when His Majesty defined it in some such words as these: 'I will not reign if I cannot do it in such a fashion as I can be answerable for to God, my conscience and my subjects. But I cannot do that if I am to rule according to the will of
5 the present majority in Parliament, and I can no longer find any ministers prepared to conduct my government without subjecting themselves and me to the Parliamentary majority. I have therefore resolved to lay down my crown' . . .

    I replied that His Majesty had been acquainted ever since May
10 with my readiness to become a Minister . . . The King asked me whether I was prepared as Minister to advocate the reorganization of the army, and when I assented he asked me further whether I would do so in opposition to the majority in Parliament and its resolutions. When I asserted my willingness he finally declared,
15 'Then it is my duty, with your help, to attempt to continue the battle, and I shall not abdicate'.

    I succeeded in convincing him that so far as he was concerned, it was not a question of liberal or conservative of this or that shade, but rather of monarchical rule or parliamentary government, and
20 that the latter must be avoided at all costs, if even by a period of dictatorship. I said: 'In this situation I shall, even if your Majesty command me to do things which I do not consider right, tell you my opinion quite openly; but if you finally persist in yours, I will rather perish with the King than forsake your Majesty in the
25 contest with the Parliamentary governments.' . . . I cherished such strong feelings of devotion and affection for William I, that the

thought of perishing with him appeared to me, under the circumstances, a natural and congenial conclusion to my life.

Bismarck left the meeting as Minister-President. The appointment was not popular. He was considered by many to be a dangerous choice as head of government, likely to lead Prussia into war abroad and dictatorship at home. He lacked experience in administration but this did not worry him. He was totally confident. In his first speech to the Parliament he held up in front of the members an olive leaf (a branch not being available), as a token of peace, but his words belied the action.

1   It is not through speeches and majority decisions that the great questions of the day are decided. That was the great mistake of 1848/9. It is by iron and blood.

This phrase, afterwards reversed to 'blood and iron', became famous. In the meantime he solved the problem of the military budget by withdrawing it, announcing that the support of Parliament for the Bill was unnecessary as the army reforms could be financed from taxation. To liberal suggestions that the people should refuse to pay taxes, Bismarck replied that he had 200 000 soldiers ready to persuade them. Parliament declared his actions illegal but he ignored it, and in the next four years the taxes were collected and the army reorganized as if the Prussian Parliament did not exist.

Bismarck's justification for this high-handed action was that he needed to ensure sufficient military power to be able to bring about a Prussian solution to the German question at the expense of Austria. Events played into his hands in 1863, and he took full advantage of them.

4 Austro-Prussian Conflict

A century earlier Prussia, Russia and Austria had divided Poland between them. Relations between Prussia and her Polish citizens had been uneasy and Poles had been blamed, without much evidence, for some of the disturbances of 1848. Bismarck thought they were troublemakers. In a private letter written to his sister in 1861 he advocated

1   Strike the Poles so that they despair for their lives. I have every sympathy for their plight, but if we want to survive we cannot but exterminate them.

In 1863 when the inhabitants of Russian Poland rose in revolt against the Tsar, Bismarck viewed the situation with concern. Trouble in any part of Poland could constitute a threat to Prussia as it could escalate into a general Polish uprising against their rulers. The Tsar, who had introduced a moderately benevolent regime into his part of Poland, was disappointed by the Poles' ingratitude and ordered the revolt to be

suppressed. France, Austria and Britain protested and offered media-
tion. There was even a threat of war. Bismarck took the opportunity to
assert himself against France and at the same time gain Russian
friendship by sending an envoy to Moscow with offers of military assistance. The Tsar refused the offer but agreed to a Convention by which
Prussia would hand over to the Russians any Polish rebels who crossed
the border.

Western anger was immediately diverted from Russia and directed
towards Prussia. Austria joined in the condemnation and Bismarck
found himself isolated. In an attempt to extricate himself, he resorted to
the pretence that the Convention did not exist because it had never been
ratified. This angered the Tsar and Prussia was left completely friend-
less. The rising was finally suppressed a year later. In the end Prussia
emerged from the affair less disastrously than Bismarck deserved or
expected. The Tsar had been deeply offended by Austrian and French
criticism, and, as a result, the danger of an Austrian-French-Russian
coalition against Prussia, which Bismarck feared, now seemed unlikely.
It was even possible that Prussia would be able to count on Russia
remaining neutral in the event of war with Austria or France.

a) *Schleswig-Holstein*

In November 1863 the childless King Frederick of Denmark died.
Frederick had also been the ruler of the two duchies of Schleswig and
Holstein which had been under Danish rule for 400 years. The population of Schleswig was mixed Danish and German, while that of Holstein was almost entirely German. Holstein was a member of the German
Confederation; Schleswig was not. There had frequently been trouble
over the Duchies, including that in 1848 when the Holsteiners had
rebelled against Denmark and Prussian troops had marched to their aid
with the loud support of the Frankfurt Parliament, until Russian intervention had forced the Prussian army into retreat.

A treaty signed in London by the Great Powers in 1852 had agreed that
Frederick would be succeeded as ruler of Denmark and of the Duchies
by Christian of Glücksburg, who was heir to the Danish throne through
marriage to the King's first cousin. Schleswig and Holstein contested his
claim on the grounds that the Salic Law operated there. This law forbade
inheritance through the female line, and the Schleswig-Holsteiners put
forward their own claimant, the Prince of Augustenburg. He, however,
did not object to being passed over in the treaty, having been well paid to
agree, although he never formally renounced his rights.

When Christian of Glücksburg became King of Denmark in November 1863, government officials in Holstein refused to swear allegiance to
him and the son of the Prince of Augustenburg now claimed both duchies
on the grounds that his father had never signed away his rights to them.
The smaller states of the German Confederation sent an army to invade

Holstein in support of Augustenburg as the rightful Duke. At the same time Bismarck persuaded Austria to take joint military action with Prussia against Denmark because King Frederick's promise to maintain the separate rights of the Duchies had been broken by Christian who had annexed Schleswig to the Danish crown.

In January 1864 a combined Prussian and Austrian army advanced through Holstein and into Schleswig. A temporary truce was arranged in April while another conference was held in London to look for a peaceful solution. It soon became clear that Britain, France and Russia had no united policy. Austria gave her support to the Augustenburg claim, while Prussia voted for Schleswig and Holstein to become a separate state, under Danish sovereignty, and for Schleswig as well as Holstein to be a member of the German Confederation. The Danes would not accept any such suggestion and the Conference was deadlocked. In June fighting started again. The struggle was unequal and the Danes surrendered.

By the Treaty of Vienna in October 1864 the King of Denmark gave up his rights over the Duchies to Austria and Prussia, to be jointly administered. Despite Austrian support for Augustenburg Bismarck had no intention of allowing him to take over the Duchies, except as a puppet ruler, and that role he would not accept. Bismarck hoped eventually to annex both Schleswig and Holstein to Prussia.

By the summer of 1865 the future of the Duchies was still not settled, and tension between Austria and Prussia was high. Austria continued to support Augustenburg's claim while Prussia worked for annexation. 'We are reaching a parting of the ways', said Bismarck. 'Unfortunately our tickets are for different lines'.

Neither country wanted war – Austria for economic reasons, as war was too expensive a luxury for an almost bankrupt country, and Prussia because Bismarck was not convinced that the Prussian army was yet ready to fight and win. It was while Bismarck and William I were 'taking the waters' at the fashionable Austrian spa town of Bad Gastein, that an Austrian envoy arrived to open negotiations and to offer concessions over the Duchies. As a result of this meeting it was provisionally agreed in August 1865 by the Convention of Gastein that the joint Austro-Prussian administration of the Duchies should be ended. The Duchy nearest to Prussia, Holstein, would be given to Austria and the other, Schleswig, to Prussia to administer, but the two powers would retain joint sovereignty over both Duchies. The 'indissoluble Duchies' were to be divided.

Historians have argued for over a century about Bismarck's motives and about his aims in dealing with the Schleswig-Holstein affair. Bismarck himself, according to the Hessian minister,

1   . . . boasted with the candour peculiar to him of how, from the beginning, he had conducted the Schleswig affair in accordance with Prussian interests. He had posed conditions to the Danes

which he knew they could not accept. At the same time by indirect
5 means he had encouraged them to active resistance. Through his
secret agents he had put before them the certain prospect of
English assistance, while he had assured himself in advance that
France did not want to go to war and therefore England had to keep
her sword in the scabbard. . . . His own aim is the annexation of
10 the Duchies, the difficulty is to bring the king to act.

* What were Bismarck's aims during the Danish campaign? Had he
used the Schleswig-Holstein crisis and its aftermath as a means of
manipulating Austria, first into co-operating with Prussia within the
Confederation in bilateral action against the Danes, and then manoeuv-
ring her into open confrontation with Prussia as a way of settling the
problem of leadership in Germany? Did he want to continue the dual
leadership, or was he considering a division of the Confederation into a
Protestant Prussian north and a Catholic Austrian south, as he suggested
in January 1866 to the Austrian Emperor? The evidence is not conclu-
sive, and many historians would suggest that, whatever he said later, he
had no clear policy at the time. It was indeed a case of 'allowing events to
ripen'.

The particular problem of the Duchies was temporarily solved, but the
more general problem of rivalry between Prussia and Austria remained.
The Danish war had convinced Bismarck that Britain and Russia were
unlikely to interfere in a war between Austria and Prussia. Italy might be
a possible ally in such a war, for she was already involved in a struggle
against Austria in northern Italy, but her military resources were limited.
The attitude of France would be all important in the isolation of Austria.
Bismarck and the French Emperor, Napoleon III, met at Biarritz in the
south of France in October 1865. The meeting was inconclusive, but
generally friendly.

b) *War with Austria*

In February 1866 at a meeting of the Prussian Crown Council Bismarck
made a clear statement that war with Austria was only a matter of time. It
would be fought not just to settle the final fate of the Duchies, but over
the wider issue of who should control Germany. He would achieve by
war what the liberals of 1848–9 had failed to achieve by peaceful means: a
united Germany. But this united Germany would be under Prussian
control.

The groundwork was carefully laid. A secret alliance was made with
Italy in April 1866, by which Victor Emmanuel, King of Italy, agreed to
follow Prussia if she declared war on Austria within three months. In
return Italy would acquire Venetia from Austria as her reward when the
war ended.

Immediately after the treaty with Italy had been signed, Bismarck started plans for war with Austria. He began by introducing in the Federal Diet plans for a reform of the Confederation. These plans were for a representative assembly elected by universal manhood suffrage. He knew that the proposal would be unacceptable to Austria and that war was not far off.

The Austrian army could not be mobilized quickly, so the Austrians, afraid of a surprise attack, were forced to take what appeared to be the aggressive step of mobilizing unilaterally in April 1866. Prussia mobilized in May, seemingly as a response to Austrian threats. The Great Powers of Britain, France and Russia proposed a Congress to discuss the situation. Bismarck felt compelled to agree; to do otherwise would put him in a weak position. But he was very relieved when Austria refused, making the Congress unworkable. He kept up a front of wanting peace by sending an envoy to Vienna, but this mission came to nothing.

The situation deteriorated further when, in early June, and in breach of previous promises, Austria referred the Schleswig-Holstein problem to the Diet. Bismarck's response was to send a Prussian army into Austrian controlled Holstein. To his surprise and disappointment this did not immediately lead to war. To stir things up, he presented to the Diet an extended version of his proposals for a reform of the Federal Constitution. The Diet's answer was to censure Prussia as an agressor for sending an army into Holstein.

* Prussia immediately withdrew from the Confederation and invited all the other German states to ally themselves with her against Austria. The next day Prussian troops marched into Hanover, Hesse-Cassel and Saxony all of which had sided with Austria in the Diet. Hesse-Cassel and Saxony offered no resistance, but Hanover fought until her army was defeated. The war had begun, without any formal declaration. It became known as the Seven Weeks' War, for that was the length of its duration.

The future of Bismarck, Prussia and Germany lay with the Prussian army. 'If we are beaten, I shall not return. I can die only once, and it befits the vanquished to die', said Bismarck, somewhat melodramatically. The Prussian army's reputation was not high, but since the shambles of 1859 reforms had been successfully carried out and the army was now under the command of General von Moltke, a gifted military leader. In co-operation with the War Minister Roon, he had reorganized and retrained the army. The command structure had also been modernized. Advance planning and preparation, particularly in the use of the railways for moving troops, meant that mobilization, while not perfect, was much more efficient than that of the Austrian army.

The Italians had fulfilled their part of the secret treaty and had followed Prussia into the war. This meant that the Austrian army was forced to fight on two fronts, in the north against the Prussians and in the south against the Italians. The Italian army was weak and inefficient and was quickly defeated by the Austrians on 24 June. To prevent the victorious Austrians in the south from linking up with their troops in the north, Moltke took the risk of crossing into Bohemia (now part of Czechoslovakia and then part of the Austrian Empire). He had three separate armies and intended to use them to surround and annihilate the Austrian army. On 2 July, the Austrian commander telegraphed to his Emperor that unless peace were made at once his army would be utterly defeated.

* Peace was not made. The next day fierce fighting took place at Sadowa, called Königgratz by the Prussians. It was a large-scale battle with nearly half a million men involved, and the two sides almost equally balanced. The Austrians were well equipped with artillery and used it effectively at the start of the battle, but they were soon caught in a Prussian pincer movement. The Prussians brought into use their new needle guns, so called from the shape of the firing pin. Its rate of fire was five times greater than anything the Austrians possessed, and it proved decisive when the Austrians counter-attacked. The Austrian army was forced to retreat in disorder. The Prussians had won the battle and with it the war because the Austrian government recognized that further fighting would almost certainly lead to further defeats and might even result in a break up of the Empire. For Austria the priority was a rapid end to the fighting at any reasonable cost. Prussia was now in a position to dictate terms as the victor. It was a personal victory too for Bismarck, and put him in a position to dominate not only Prussia, but also the whole of Germany in the next quarter of a century.

He returned to Berlin with the King, Moltke and his hundred captured Austrian guns to a hero's welcome. A grateful Prussia, most of whose people had been no more than lukewarm about the war not believing that Austria would be defeated, presented him with a reward of £60 000, with which he bought a run down estate at Varzin in Pomerania. His wife hated the place, especially the house which she referred to as a 'crooked horror', and it was only used for a few weeks in the year. He was promoted to Major General in honour of the victory. It had been noticeable that at meetings of the 'war cabinet' he had been the only one present wearing civilian clothes. Any uniform he was then entitled to would have marked him as an officer of lower rank than anyone else there, and he could not have borne that. Now he was a high ranking officer he could flaunt his uniform on an equal footing, and he never again appeared in public except in full dress uniform. He had earned his spurs and intended to wear them in a Prussia, and later a Germany, dominated by military power.

The road to Vienna lay open after the victory at Königgratz. Austria was at the mercy of Prussia. William I had previously been unwilling to wage wholehearted war on a fellow monarch, but he now proposed an advance on Vienna and a takeover of Austria. Bismarck who claimed that he wanted to keep defeated Austria intact as a possible future ally, persuaded him to give up these ideas. At a noisy and angry meeting of the 'war cabinet' on 23 July, William I and his senior generals raged against

Bismarck's policy of not annexing any Austrian territory, while Bismarck himself was in a state of nervous collapse and floods of tears in an adjoining room, threatening suicide if his advice was not taken. In the end Bismarck's decision stood. No Austrian territory was to be taken over by Prussia.

5 Prussian Ascendancy

An armistice was signed between Prussia and Austria in July and was followed by a peace treaty, the Peace of Prague, in August. The terms of the treaty were mainly concerned with the remodelling of North Germany as Prussia wished. Prussia annexed a good deal of territory, including at last both Schleswig and Holstein, as well as Hesse-Cassel, Hanover, Nassau and Frankfurt, along with their four million inhabitants. All other German states north of the River Main, including Saxony, were to be formed into a North German Confederation under Prussian leadership (see map on page 80).

The states south of the River Main were to be made into a separate independent union. Bismarck began by demanding territory and large sums of money from these states as compensation for their support of Austria during the war. When these demands were refused he was unwilling to proceed to open annexation, mainly because of the known opposition of Napoleon III to such action (see page 67). He therefore proposed secret alliances between the four southern states and Prussia. These were agreed. They provided that if Prussia were attacked the four states would not only fight alongside Prussia, but would put their armies under the command of the King of Prussia. This meant giving up their military independence. Why the states agreed so readily is not certain. They seem to have been sufficiently afraid of Bismarck to feel safer in some sort of alliance with him. They may also have believed that such an alliance would protect them against a possible French attack.

In Italy Austria surrendered Venetia. It was ironic that the only territory, apart from Holstein, lost by Austria at the end of the Seven Weeks' War was in Italy, where she had not been defeated, and had in fact won two substantial victories, one on land at the start of the war and another later on at sea, which destroyed the Italian navy.

* Why was Bismarck so moderate, when Prussia could have taken over all of Germany and most of Austria? Before the war ended he had written to the King of Prussia urging William to make an early peace with Austria:

1 We have to avoid wounding Austria too severely; we have to avoid leaving behind in her unnecessary bitterness of feeling or desire for revenge, we ought to keep the possibility of becoming friends again. If Austria were severely injured, she would become the ally
5 of France and of every other opponent of ours. . . . German

Austria we could neither wholly nor partly make use of. The acquisition of provinces like Austrian Silesia and part of Bohemia could not strengthen the Prussian state; it would not lead to an amalgamation of German Austria with Prussia, and Vienna could 10 not be governed by Berlin as a mere dependency.

His argument was that Prussia might need Austria's friendship one day in the future so it would be unwise to upset her by too harsh a treaty. In any case a harsh treaty would throw Austria into the arms of France, and this could lead to a coalition against Prussia. Bismarck was almost paranoid about the possibility of an anti-Prussian coalition, and he had been in a panic about the likelihood of one during the Seven Weeks' War. He need not have worried then, for the Tsar of Russia was not ready for war in 1866 and Napoleon was still thinking about what to do when the Prussian victory was announced.

Before the peace treaty was signed in August 1866, Napoleon had agreed, reluctantly, to a Prussian north Germany. His fear of a united Germany, threatening French security, was allayed by the proposal to set up an independent south German union, and he was happily in ignorance of Bismarck's military alliances with the southern states made even before the treaty was signed.

a) *The North German Confederation*

In North Germany the Prussian takeover met with general disapproval. It was not unification, but conquest. Hesse-Cassel, Nassau, Hanover, Frankfurt and Schleswig-Holstein were not consulted; they were just annexed.

Bismarck had shown a calculated moderation and clemency in his treatment of Austria. He showed neither of these to his fellow north Germans. The wealthy city of Frankfurt had not opposed Prussia during the war, but was taken over just the same. The city was starved into surrender and was fined the enormous sum of 25 million guilders, with one million guilders interest for every day the fine remained unpaid. The burgomaster hanged himself. The aged King of Hanover was driven out, his personal fortune confiscated (it came in useful to Bismarck later when it was used to bribe the King of Bavaria), and his kingdom taken over by Prussia. The small states of Hesse-Cassel and Nassau were actually incorporated into Prussia itself as their annexation helped to consolidate Prussia geographically.

Those north German states, such as Saxony, not annexed by Prussia were left with some independence within the North German Confederation. Some historians have seen this as a trial run by Bismarck in North Germany for an eventual wider federation taking in all *Kleindeutschland*. They argue that as he had no scruples he could easily have annexed the remaining northern states if he had so wished and did not do so because he wanted to show those Germans south of the Main not only how considerate an ally Prussia could be to those states which co-operated with her, but also how advantageous membership of a Prussian-controlled federation could be. This argument does not seem very convincing. More credible is the suggestion that he saw no advantage to Prussia in too speedy a takeover of too many states at once. Such action would only lead to a dilution of Prussian culture and traditions. Instead of Prussia absorbing Germany, Germany would end up absorbing Prussia.

* At the end of 1866 Bismarck began drafting the constitution for the North German Confederation, which came into effect in July 1867. The North German Confederation lasted only four years, but its constitution was to continue, largely unaltered, as the constitution of the German Empire. It established a federal unity between the individual states (first in the Confederation and afterwards in the Empire) and the central authority.

The states, including of course Prussia, had substantial rights, keeping their own rulers and being governed by their own laws and constitutions with their own parliamentary assemblies. They had their own legal and administrative systems, and local taxation met the cost of government services, provided education and supported the Church.

The central authority lay with the *Bundesrat* (the Federal Council) in which the states were represented by delegates who acted on the instructions of their governments. The number of delegates was fixed in relation to the size of the state; out of 43 votes Prussia had 17, Saxony four and most of the others one each. Decisions were made by a simple majority vote and, in practice, Prussia was never outvoted in the *Bundesrat*. The King of Prussia was President of the North German Confederation and also the commander-in-chief, and had the power of declaring war and making peace.

As well as the *Bundesrat* the constitution provided for the election of a *Reichstag* (parliament) by universal manhood suffrage. The Federal Chancellor (the Chief Minister) was not responsible to the *Reichstag* nor did he need majority support in it. He was responsible only to the President of the Confederation, who could appoint or dismiss the Chancellor. The first Reichstag was elected in February 1867. The largest single party in it were the National Liberals and they gained a number of concessions from Bismarck, now the Federal Chancellor. These included a secret instead of an open ballot at elections, and the right to pass an annual budget. This financial control was very limited because it did not include control over the military budget, which accounted for about 90 per cent of the Confederation's spending. The liberals and Bismarck struggled over the question of the military budget and eventually reached a compromise. It would remain outside the *Reichstags'* control for five years, until 1872. Then the amount of money to be spent on the army would be fixed by law and for this the *Reichstag's* consent would be required. All laws needed approval of the *Reichstag*, the *Bundesrat* and the King of Prussia as President of the Confederation.

They also needed the signature of the Chancellor. The *Bundesrat* and the *Reichstag* could both initiate legislation.

Bismarck was always opposed to the idea of parliamentary government on the British model, which reduced the crown to symbolic status and put power in the hands of parliament. His declared view of the political abilities of his fellow Germans was very low:

1 Considering the political incapacity of the average German, the parliamentary system would lead to conditions such as had prevailed in 1848, that is to say weakness and incompetence at the top and ever new demands from below.

It is unexpected therefore, to find Bismarck responsible for insisting on universal manhood suffrage in the election of the *Reichstag*. It may have been merely a gesture to placate the liberals. Certainly, the democratic manner of the election did not compensate for the great weakness of the *Reichstag*, that ministers, including the Chancellor, were not members of it and were not responsible to it.

* The Battle of Königgratz was not Bismarck's only victory in 1866. On the home front he had his successes too. On the same day as the battle was won, elections were held in Prussia. Patriotic war fever resulted in a big increase in the number of conservatives elected to the Prussian Parliament. The numbers jumped from 34 to 142, while the liberal parties were reduced from 253 to 148. After news of the victory and after the terms of the peace treaty were announced many liberals changed their attitude to Bismarck. 'Blood and Iron' had succeeded as he had promised, where liberals had failed in 1849.

Unification was happening, even if it was being carried out by force, and some liberals were prepared to believe that the end justified the means. A new era of harmony began between Bismarck and the liberals in the Prussian Parliament. Only seven votes were cast against an Indemnity Bill introduced by Bismarck at the beginning of the new session. This Bill asked Parliament to grant an 'Indemnity' for any actions committed or payments made by the government during the previous four years without Parliament's consent. He appealed for better relations between Parliament and the government:

1 We [the royal government] wish for peace in this domestic conflict.
In our view the Fatherland needs it at the present moment more than ever before.

He spoke of the need for the government to work jointly with Parliament to build a new Germany. It was an implicit acceptance of Parliamentary rights.

In the first flush of enthusiasm and united in patriotic sentiment, the Parliament voted large sums of money to the victorious generals, but this unity did not last. Both the left- and right-wing parties in Parliament split into new groupings. A large section of the old Liberal Party formed themselves into the National Liberal Party, pledged to support Bismarck in his nationalist policy, but equally pledged to maintain liberal constitutional principles against any government attempt to undermine them, and to support free trade. On the right, the *Junker* Party opposed Bismarck as a wild revolutionary and a traitor to his class, whittling away at the royal prerogative and losing Prussia's identity in the new unified North Germany. Those conservatives who were less reactionary than the *Junkers* formed a new party group, the Free Conservatives. They, together with the National Liberals, were to provide the support which Bismarck needed to carry out his policies.

Bismarck's triumph in 1866 forced Austria to withdraw from German affairs and left the field clear for Prussian influence to dominate. The German Confederation of 1815 was finally dead.

Making notes on 'Prussia and Austria 1849–66'

Your notes on this chapter should make clear the changing relationship between Prussia and Austria in this period, during which the balance of power was reversed. Austria was supreme in 1849 after the failure of the revolutions and of the Frankfurt Parliament. In the 1850s there was growing political and economic rivalry between the two Powers. In 1862 Otto von Bismarck was appointed Minister President of Prussia. Under his leadership Austria was totally defeated in the Seven Weeks' War of 1866, and the North German Confederation was established.

The following headings and subheadings should help you:
1.   Austrian Ascendancy
1.1. The Prussian Union Plan
1.2. Hesse-Cassel
1.3. Olmütz
1.4. Economic developments
1.5. Contrast between Prussia and Austria
2.   Prussia
2.1. Manteuffel
2.2. William I
2.3. The Army Bill
3.   Bismarck
3.1. Early life
3.2. Character
3.3. Political beginnings
3.4. Political ideas before 1862
3.5. Appointment as Minister President
3.6. Action on the Army Bill
4.   Austrio-Prussian Conflict
4.1. Poland
4.2. Schleswig-Holstein

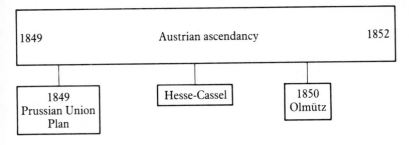

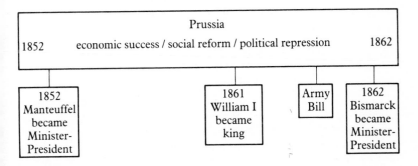

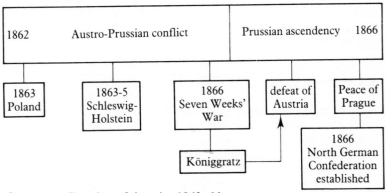

Summary – Prussia and Austria, 1849–66

4.3. Bismarck's aims
4.4. Preparation for war
4.5. The Seven Weeks' War
4.6. Königgratz
5.   Prussian Ascendancy

Answering essay questions on 'Prussia and Austria 1849–66'

Evidence from this chapter will be needed to answer the general questions on the unification of Germany discussed on page 105.

You may sometimes find yourself facing a question specifically on the relationship between Prussia and Austria in the struggle for the control of Germany. For example:

> Why had Prussia, rather than Austria, achieved dominance in Germany by 1866? (Oxford and Cambridge, 1983).

This is a straightforward 'Why' question. The temptation is to draw up a chronological list of points, beginning with Austrian superiority, moving onto the the rivalry of the 1850s and ending with the Prussian victory of 1866. Unless you are very careful the danger is that you will end up writing a narrative essay rather than an analytical one. It is better to look for another way of grouping your points which is not based on chronology. One obvious possibility is by broad aspects, such as military, economic or political.

Plan an answer to the question using these three broad aspects. Under each one, list the points you would make. Then decide what evidence you would include to substantiate each point. In what order would you consider the broad aspects? Why?

Source-based questions on 'Prussia and Austria, 1849–66'

1   Bismarck as a young man and before his rise to power
Read carefully the description of Bismarck while at university given on page 47, and study the portrait and the photograph of Bismarck in 1858 on page 50. Answer the following questions:
a) What tentative conclusions about Bismarck's values and attitudes as a young man could be drawn from the description of him while at university? Support your conclusions with evidence.
b) The artist of the portrait has presented Bismarck in a way that is designed to evoke a particular response from the viewer. What is this response? Explain your answer.
c) Given that the portrait was acceptable to Bismarck, what does it indicate about his values and attitudes?
d) What are the strengths and weaknesses of the portrait and the

photograph as evidence about Bismarck in 1858?
e) In what respects do the three pieces of evidence i) support and ii) contradict each other?

2 Bismarck's appointment as Minister-President, 1862
Read carefully Bismarck's description of his meeting with William I, given on pages 51–2. Answer the following questions:
a) Why had the King decided to abdicate, (lines 1–8)?
b) How did Bismarck make him change his mind?
c) For what reasons might a historian doubt the accuracy of this account?
d) The account may not give an accurate impression of what happened during the meeting. But it could be regarded as providing clear evidence on some things. What things are these? Explain your answer.

3 Bismarck's views on war
Read carefully the short extracts from Bismarck's speech to the Erfurt Parliament, (page 52), from his first speech as Minister-President, (page 52), and from his comments on the Poles, (page 52). Answer the following questions:
a) Summarize Bismarck's views on the use of war, as presented in the three short extracts.
b) What reasons are there for doubting that the extracts represent Bismarck's real views?

4 Bismarck and Schleswig-Holstein
Read carefully the extract from the report of the Hessian minister, given on pages 54–5. Answer the following questions:
a) Which interpretation of Bismarck's policy over Schleswig-Holstein does the extract support?
b) What evidence about Bismarck's character does the extract contain?
c) Why should the extract not be taken at face value?

5 Bismarck and Austria
Read carefully the extract from Bismarck's letter to William I in 1866 given on pages 58–9. Answer the following questions:
a) Bismarck gives two major reasons for not annexing Austrian territory. What are they?
b) What evidence does the extract contain about Bismarck's interpretation of the phrase 'German nationalism'.
c) Bismarck often expressed contradictory views on the same topic. This means that his statements must be corroborated with other evidence as far as possible. Is it likely that Bismarck genuinely held the views expressed in the letter? Explain your answer.

CHAPTER 4

Prussia and France 1862–71

1 War with Austria

Bismarck had visited Paris for the World Fair in 1855 and while there had met the Emperor Napoleon III. This first meeting was a successful one on a personal level, and the two men parted on friendly terms. Their paths were to cross throughout the 1860s in very varied circumstances, and their final meeting – to discuss the French surrender in 1870 – took place in a very different atmosphere from the first.

Nephew of Napoleon I, Louis Napoleon had a hectic and colourful early career. He was involved in revolutionary activities, held liberal sympathies, belonged to secret societies, was imprisoned, escaped, plotted and intrigued throughout Europe. In 1848 he was elected President of the French Republic, but overthrew it in December 1852 and made himself Emperor of France as Napoleon III at the age of 44, when his health was already beginning to fail.

The motives behind Napoleon III's foreign policy are somewhat difficult to determine. He seems to have wanted simply to restore France to a position of influence in Europe, through peaceful means if possible. But the difficulty he had in making a decision and sticking to it made him appear inconsistent and unpredictable. Unlike his uncle, Napoleon I, he lacked the ruthlessness and the will to carry things through to their logical conclusion.

This put him at a marked disadvantage when dealing with a man as devious and determined as Bismarck, who was likely to outplay him at his own game. Yet the logic of the international situation in the early 1860s suggested that the two men could act in close association with one another. Both wanted to overturn the territorial arrangements made at Vienna in 1815 and there was sufficient 'available' land for both to make gains. Therefore Bismarck soon turned to France as Prussia's obvious ally of the future.

* After the long drawn out Schleswig-Holstein affair had apparently been concluded by the agreement made at Gastein in 1865 between Prussia and Austria (see page 54), Bismarck began to search for allies in a possible war with Austria. He saw little chance of Britain or Russia taking any active part in such a war. That left Italy, recently united, or France. To sound out Napoleon's feelings, Bismarck went to his second meeting with the Emperor, this time at Biarritz, in October 1865. The exact details of the conversation are unknown. Bismarck's own version is sketchy and vague and is little help. Historians have speculated ever since on what passed between them. Maybe Bismarck made a deal with Napoleon by agreeing on territorial or other rewards for French neutrality in the event of an Austria-Prussian war, but it is unlikely that

Bismarck with his preference for keeping his options open, would have committed himself so far in advance. More probably he suggested vaguely that an opportunity might arise for French expansion, perhaps in the Rhineland, after a Prussian victory over Austria. Almost certainly there was no commitment on either side, but there probably were protestations of good will and general support. After all, Bismarck had remarked earlier in the year that 'Prussia and France are the two states in Europe whose interests make them most mutually dependent'.

* In early 1866, when a secret treaty was drawn up between Prussia and Italy by which the Italians agreed to follow Prussia if she declared war on Austria in return for receiving Austrian-controlled Venetia as a reward once Austria was defeated, Bismarck turned again to Napoleon. Victor Emmanuel, King of Italy, had refused to sign the treaty unless Napoleon agreed. Napoleon gave his agreement and the treaty was signed in April 1866.

Bismarck began to have some doubts about Napoleon's intentions. He was not certain that he could rely on Napoleon's protestations of neutrality. He was right, for Napoleon was sending supportive messages to Vienna as well as to Berlin. He was hedging his bets, by keeping on good terms with both Prussia and Austria and at the same time pursuing his own goals. He had already made sure that Italy would receive Venetia if Prussia won, thereby assisting her to acquire the territory he had failed to win for her as promised during the war with Austria in 1859. So to make equally sure that the same thing would happen if Austria won, he made a secret treaty with Austria in June. In return for Austria agreeing to give up Venetia when Prussia had been defeated, Napoleon promised to remain neutral and to try to persuade Italy to remain neutral also in any war between Austria and Prussia. It is probable that Napoleon hoped to be able to turn his neutrality to good advantage by mediating between the combatants and by threatening to join in the war to persuade them to make peace on his terms, which would include territorial gains for France.

* The speed of Prussia's victory in the Seven Weeks' War (see pages 56–7) made it impossible for Napoleon to carry through his intentions. When he attempted to mediate after the Battle of Königgratz, the offer was declined by Bismarck who instead sent the Prussian ambassador in Paris to inform Napoleon that Prussian expansion would be limited to north Germany, and that the south German states would remain independent. This planned division of Germany was presented to Napoleon as a reward for his neutrality during the war because Bismarck realized that Napoleon would regard a united Germany as a potential threat to France. Bismarck explained in his *Reminiscences*, written nearly 30 years later, that he felt it necessary to appease Napoleon and leave Germany divided, because he thought that probably Napoleon was pro-Austrian, and was about to join a coalition with Austria against Prussia before a peace treaty could be concluded. For the same reason, he

claimed, he made sure that Austria was generously treated in the peace settlement, as this would make it less likely that Austria would seek revenge in the future by allying herself with France, or 'any other enemy' of Prussia. Most historians would doubt that Bismarck had the situation as carefully thought out as this at the time.

* The Treaty of Prague was signed on 23 August 1866 and confirmed for Napoleon that he would not face a united Germany north and south of the River Main. The south German states had been guaranteed an 'independent international position'. It appeared that Napoleon III had achieved something by his neutrality but of course the guarantees were not worth the paper they were written on, for Bismarck had gone behind Napoleon's back and made military alliances with the south German states even before the treaty was signed (see page 58).

Soon afterwards Bismarck extended the *Zollverein* to include the four southern states and involved them in the new *Zollparlament*, or customs parliament. Although it was nominally concerned only with economic affairs, Bismarck hoped that the *Zollparlament*, as a Prussian dominated institution covering all *Kleindeutschland* would in due course turn its attention to non-commercial business as well. It would be a further step in the Prussian domination of Germany, another way for him to control a Germany united in fact if not in theory.

Even if Bismarck had not planned to unite Germany north and south of the River Main, it is highly probable that it would eventually have come about, whatever Napoleon wanted. The North German Confederation and Prussia represented more than two thirds of Germany, now that Austria had been excluded, and it was unrealistic to suppose that the remaining third could or would continue an independent existence indefinitely.

The four south German states did not present a united front, for they distrusted each other as much as they distrusted Bismarck. In addition they distrusted Napoleon. They believed he had had designs on part of their territory as his reward for French neutrality during the war and as compensation for agreeing to an extension of Prussian power in Germany. They knew that he hankered after an area on the west bank of the River Rhine, which under Napoleon I had been part of France until 1814. In July 1866 the French ambassador in Berlin had presented detailed plans to Bismarck for France to acquire part of the Rhineland belonging to Bavaria and Hesse. This would restore the French frontier to the 1814 line.

The idea was firmly rejected by Bismarck who did not want to give away any German territory to France. But he also did not want to alienate Napoleon. He therefore suggested that France should look for compensation, not in the German-speaking Rhineland, but further north in the French-speaking areas of Belgium and Luxemburg. Napoleon accepted the idea and decided to concentrate on Luxemburg.

2 The Luxemburg Crisis

Napoleon went ahead at once with efforts to acquire Luxemburg. He needed some quick and showy success to counter-balance Prussia's recent victories and Luxemburg, though small, would be better than nothing.

Bismarck's policy on the Luxemburg question is difficult to unravel. He began by helping Napoleon to 'persuade' the King of the Netherlands, who was also Duke of Luxemburg, to relinquish the Duchy. The King readily agreed. Perhaps memories of the Schleswig-Holstein affair had something to do with it, for Prussia had certain rights in the Duchy of Luxemburg, in particular to garrison the fortress. This right dated from the Vienna Settlement of 1815, which had made the fortress part of the German Confederation.

But by the end of 1866 Bismarck was feeling much less need to be friendly towards Napoleon, who was stirring up demonstrations in Luxemburg against 'the hated domination of Prussia' as part of his campaign in the Duchy. This created much anti-French feeling in Germany. Partly in response to this and partly to encourage nationalist feelings Bismarck now began to refer to Luxemburg as German, and announced that its surrender to France would be 'a humiliating injury to German national feelings'. He denied any responsibility by Prussia for the agreement between Holland and France. He invoked nationalism: 'If a nation *feels* its honour has been violated, it has in fact been violated and appropriate action must ensue. . . . We must in my opinion risk war rather than yield.' Anti-French sentiment continued to increase throughout Germany.

Why did Bismarck encourage this nationalist hysteria? Not to start a war with France, for he did not believe that the Prussian army was as yet strong enough, and he knew that the North German Confederation was still fragile. His intention perhaps was to start a campaign of provocation to drive Napoleon into war in due course or perhaps it was just that he now realized that he was in a strong enough diplomatic position to stop France making any territorial gains. In a long interview which Bismarck gave to a British journalist in September 1867 he spoke of his wish for peace:

1   There is nothing in our attitude to annoy or alarm France. . . .
there is nothing to prevent the maintenance of peace for ten or fifteen years, by which time the French will have become accustomed to German unity, and will consequently have ceased to
5 care about it.
    I told our generals this spring, when they endeavoured to prove to me, by all sorts of arguments that we must beat the French if we went to war then, 'I will still do all I can to prevent war; for you must remember, gentlemen, a war between such near neighbours

10 and old enemies as France and Prussia, however it may turn out, is
only the first of at least six; and supposing we gained all six, what
should we have succeeded in doing? Why, in ruining France
certainly, and most likely ourselves into the bargain. Do you think
a poor, bankrupt, starving, ragged neighbour is as desirable as a
15 wealthy, solvent, fat, well clothed one? France buys largely from
us, and sells us a great many things we want. Is it in our interest to
ruin her completely?' I strove for peace then, and I will do so as
long as maybe; only, remember German susceptibilities must be
respected, or I cannot answer for the people – not even for the
20 King!

In this interview Bismarck presented himself as a man of peace. He
wanted to allay British fears about Prussian warlike intentions and to
reduce the chance of a British alliance with France. He made use of
methods like this interview with a responsible and respected foreign
journalist to present himself and his policies in a favourable light to those
whom he wished to influence. He understood very well the use of
propaganda and the value of a good public relations system. This makes
it difficult to identify his motives or to arrive at the truth about his
intentions from his public utterances. He did not always believe what he
said, or say what he believed.

While Bismarck was declaiming his pacific intentions and playing
down the danger of war, Napoleon III was in trouble and under attack at
home. He needed to raise his prestige and unwisely proclaimed that only
his intervention had halted the Prussian advance on Vienna after the
battle of Königgratz. Bismarck took umbrage at the implications that
his actions were controlled by Napoleon, and in March 1867 he released
texts of the secret military alliances he had made with the South German
states before the Treaty of Prague. These showed that the North German
Confederation and the states to the south of the River Main were not as
independent of each other as had been assumed.

* Napoleon and Bismarck now met head on in a series of diplomatic
battles. Napoleon began new negotiations with the King of the Netherlands, playing on the King's fears that Prussia was after a slice of Dutch
territory, and offering to protect the Netherlands in return for Luxemburg. From Napoleon's point of view the King wrecked the scheme by
agreeing to sell Luxemburg for 5 million guilders, subject to approval by
the King of Prussia! This, he must have known, was not likely to be
given. Indeed, Bismarck used the patriotic German fervour he had
encouraged as an excuse to threaten the King of the Netherlands not to
give up Luxemburg, and Napoleon lost any chance he might have had of
acquiring the Duchy.

Bismarck appealed to the Great Powers to settle the question. A
conference was held in London at which Luxemburg was declared
neutral, under a collective guarantee. The terms of the guarantee were

not very strong, but they did keep the French out of Luxemburg. The Prussian garrison was withdrawn, and the Luxemburg question was settled, but Franco-German relations had been seriously damaged.

The Luxemburg crisis has been described by some historians as the point at which Bismarck stopped being a Prussian patriot and became a German one. There is no evidence that Bismarck himself thought this. He stirred up and used German national feelings quite cynically as a means to increase Prussian influence over the rest of the German states, as well as a weapon against France. He was, however, aware that without some external intervention the unification of Germany under Prussia was unlikely to happen overnight. He spoke of 25 years as a probable time scale.

When he floated his new idea in 1870 that the King of Prussia should take the title of Kaiser (or Emperor) of Germany, it was turned down by the rulers of the other German states. The *Zollverein* and *Zollparlament* had done valuable work for economic unity, but political unity was as far off as ever.

Some historians believe that Bismarck came to the opinion about this time that, whatever he might say in public to the contrary, a full-scale foreign war was needed to raise national consciousness and bring the people together. As if on cue the Hohenzollern candidature crisis developed.

3 War with France

a) *Hohenzollern Candidature Crisis*

In 1868 the reigning Queen of Spain, Isabella, was driven out of the country by a revolution. The government was carried on by the Minister of War, while efforts were made to find a new monarch among the royal houses of Europe. The offer of the Spanish crown had been turned down by one Prince after another, when an approach was made to Prince Leopold of Hohenzollern. The senior branch of his family was the Prussian royal house. Bismarck always claimed that he had nothing to do with the matter until the crisis broke in July 1870, and that before then it was entirely a Hohenzollern family affair. Yet as early as May 1869, when there were rumours that the throne was being offered to Prince Leopold, Bismarck was involved in denying them.

In February 1870 an official offer was made to Prince Leopold by the Spanish government. His father referred the request to William I who as King of Prussia was head of the Hohenzollern family. William left to himself would have refused consent. He knew that to proceed would provoke French hostility, for Napoleon would see it as a threat to 'encircle' France, with Hohenzollern monarchs in Berlin and Madrid pursuing anti-French policies simultaneously. William was persuaded to change his mind by Bismarck, who sent him a strongly worded memorandum: 'It is in Germany's political interest that the house of Hohenzollern should gain in esteem and an exalted position in the world'. In the end the King gave his consent, provided that Leopold himself wished to accept the throne. As Leopold did not want to do so, the affair appeared to be at an end.

But Bismarck had secretly sent envoys to Spain, accompanied by large sums of money as bribes to push Leopold's candidacy. He also put pressure on the Hohenzollern family, as a result of which Leopold decided to accept after all. In June William, although annoyed at these underhand dealings, gave his unconditional consent.

Bismarck had planned that the document giving Leopold's acceptance would arrive in Spain, be immediately presented to the *Cortes*, the Spanish Parliament, for ratification, and then the news be announced amid general rejoicing. Unfortunately the message relayed through the Prussian embassy in Madrid suffered an unforeseen mix-up of dates due to a cipher clerk's error. As a result the *Cortes* was not in session when the document arrived and before it could be recalled the secret of Leopold's acceptance leaked out.

The news reached Paris on 3 July. This was not in accordance with Bismarck's plan. Napoleon should not have heard the news until the *Cortes* had elected Leopold and the whole matter had been settled. An angry telegram was sent to Berlin asking whether the Prussian government had known of Leopold's candidacy and declaring that 'the interests and honour of France are now in peril'. The French ambassador in Berlin was instructed to go to Ems, where Willaim I was taking the waters, to put the French case that Leopold's candidacy was a danger to France and to the European balance of power, and to advise William to stop Leopold leaving for Spain if he wanted to avoid war.

William was distressed by events and assured the ambassador of Prussia's friendship for France, for the last thing he wanted to see was war over Leopold. On 12 July Leopold's father withdrew his son's candidacy. Once again the affair appeared to have been settled, with the diplomatic honours going to France. Bismarck, in Berlin, spoke of humiliation, and threatened resignation. In the nick of time he was saved from having to make good his threat.

The French foolishly overplayed their hand. Leopold's renunciation had been announced in a telegram from his father to the Spanish government. Now the French demanded an official renunciation from William I, on behalf of Leopold, for all time, and the French ambassador was ordered to see the King again and obtain his personal assurance. On 13 July they met in the park at Ems. At first the exchange was cordial, but the tone of the conversation changed when William refused to give the assurances demanded. Not satisfied, the French government ordered the French ambassador to see William yet again and obtain an apology for having ever agreed to support Leopold's candidacy.

b) *The Ems Telegram*

That evening, in Berlin, Bismarck received a telegram from Ems, sent by the King's secretary, and describing the morning meeting between William and Count Benedetti, the French ambassador. Much later, in his *Reminiscences*, Bismarck wrote:

1 I invited Generals von Moltke and von Roon to have dinner with me on July 13th and spoke to them about my views and intentions. During the dinner conversation it was reported to me that a coded telegram had been received from Ems and was then in the process
5 of being decoded. I then read it to my guests, who were so depressed that they refused to eat or drink. All considerations, conscious and unconscious, strengthened my opinion that war could only be avoided at the cost of the honour of Prussia and of the national confidence in her.

The telegram, which so upset Bismarck and his guests, read:

1 His Majesty writes to me: 'Count Benedetti [the French ambassador] spoke to me on the promenade to demand from me, finally in a very importunate manner, that I should authorize him to telegraph at once that I bound myself for all future time never
5 again to give my consent if the Hohenzellerns should renew their candidature. I refused at last somewhat sternly, as it is neither right nor proper to undertake engagements of this kind for all time. I told him that I had as yet received no news, and as he was earlier informed from Paris and Madrid than myself, he could see clearly
10 that my government had no more interest in the matter.' His Majesty has since received a letter from Prince Charles Anthony [Leopold's father]. His Majesty, having told Count Benedetti that he was awaiting news from the Prince, has decided not to receive Count Benedetti again, but only to let him be informed through an
15 aide-de-camp: 'That his Majesty has now received from the Prince confirmation of the news which Benedetti had already received from Paris, and had nothing further to say to the ambassador'. His Majesty leaves it to your Excellency to decide whether Benedetti's fresh demand and its rejection should be at once communicated to
20 our ambassadors, to foreign nations and to the press'.

Having read the telegram, Bismarck, 'in the presence of my two guests, reduced the telegram by striking out words, but without adding or altering anything'.

The new version read:

1 After the news of the renunciation of the Hereditary Prince of Hohenzollern had been officially communicated to the Imperial government of France by the Royal Government of Spain, the French ambassador further demanded of His Majesty the King, at

5   Ems, that he would authorize him to telegraph to Paris that His
Majesty the King bound himself for all time never again to give his
consent, should the Hohenzollerns renew their candidacy. His
Majesty the King, thereupon decided not to receive the French
ambassador again, and sent the aide-de-camp on duty to tell him
10 that His Majesty had nothing further to communicate to the
ambassador.

The shortening of the text of the telegram had the effect of making the
King's message through an aide-de-camp to the French ambassador
appear to be his immediate and uncompromising response to the French
demand to renounce support for the Hohenzollern candidature for all
time. Bismarck in his *Memoirs* continued to describe his actions:

1   The difference in the effect of the abbreviated text of the Ems
telegram as compared with that produced by the original was not
the result of stronger words, but of the form, which made this
announcement appear decisive, while the original version would
5   only have been regarded as a fragment of a negotiation still pending
and to be continued at Berlin. After I had read out the concentrated
version to my two guests, Moltke remarked. 'Now it has a different
ring, in its original form it sounded like a parley; now it is like a
flourish in answer to a challenge'. I went on to explain: 'If in
10 execution of His Majesty's order, I at once communicate this text,
which contains no alteration or addition to the telegram, not only to
the newspapers but by telegraph to all our embassies it will be
known in Paris before midnight . . . and will have the effect of a red
rag on the French bull. Fight we must if we do not want to act the
15 part of the vanquished without a battle. Success, however, depends
essentially upon the impression which the origination of the war
makes upon us and others: it is important that we should be the
ones attacked'.

Bismarck personally handed the amended text of the Ems telegram to
the newspapers for publication in a special edition in Berlin and sent it for
publication abroad. Prussian embassies received copies by telegraph
with instructions to communicate the contents to foreign governments.
By morning the news was on the streets of Paris. The alterations had
made the King's actions seem more abrupt and dismissive than they
really were, and when William saw the published version he is said to
have remarked with a shudder, 'This is war'.

* How far was the Ems telegram responsible for the outbreak of war
with France? Bismarck made use of the opportunity it provided to make
war more immediate, but he had probably decided that a war with
France was needed to ensure German national unity. He had made
enquiries in the south German states, and received promises of support
in the event of war with France. He had also prepared, though not yet

submitted, a request to the *Reichstag* to initiate a war with France, if the French did not act first. The King's refusal to give into French demands made it difficult for the French to retreat without loss of face. The Ems telegram, as amended by Bismarck, was just the last straw. France had to be pushed into declaring war. It was important to Bismarck that France should appear to be the aggressor. He could then claim that Prussia had been attacked and call upon the south German states for support in accordance with the terms of their military alliances with Prussia.

Historians have argued about how far ahead Bismarck planned this confrontation. It seems probable that he had had in mind since 1866 an eventual war against France, as long as it could appear to be a defensive war, brought about by French aggression. Such a war would serve as nothing else could to bring the south German states into the Prussian fold. He was well aware that war is a great national unifier. All that was needed was a suitable opportunity. This occurred with the Hohenzollern candidature crisis, and Bismarck took full advantage of it. He was perhaps fortunate in his adversaries, for the French played into his hands with their demands for total renunciation by William I of the Hohenzollern claim. He took the chance offered, and manipulated the situation by cynically amending the Ems telegram to provoke French hostility.

* The French declaration was contained in a document which rehearsed all the events at Ems and the contents of the telegram as received in Paris. It dwelt on the threat of French security posed by 'the project of placing a Prussian Prince on the Spanish throne and the consequent need to take immediate steps for the defence of French honour and injured interests'.

Bismarck on the same day sent copies of the French declaration of war with a memorandum to all diplomatic agents of the North German Confederation with orders to circulate it to the governments to which they were accredited:

1   We summarily answer . . . that His Majesty the King, having full respect for the independence and autonomy of the Spanish nation, and for the freedom of decision of the Prince of the Hohenzollern House, never thought of putting Prince Leopold on that throne.

5   . . . War which Prussia could never have thought of, was imposed by France. The whole civilized world will admit the motives put forward by France do not exist.

c) *The Franco-Prussian War*

European historians are not in agreement about what to call the war – should it be Franco-Prussian (the usually accepted name) or Franco-German? In different ways it was both. It was the first genuinely German war, fought by the newly defined *Kleindeutschland*, but it was so dominated by Prussian expertise that it was little more than an extended

Prussian military enterprise. Bismarck and Moltke organized the German war effort and Prussian troops greatly outnumbered all other troops in the army. But, unlike 1866, all the German states fought under Prussia, presenting a united front, even if at the beginning some support was less than enthusiastic.

By the end of the war this had changed, and all Germany was united by a blind hatred of France and all things French. This was brought about by government propaganda, and particularly by Bismarck's inflammatory speeches, letters and newspaper articles. This enmity remained after the peace treaty as one of the permanent legacies of the war.

It was a war with only two combatant nations: Germany and France. Russia had promised to fight alongside Prussia if Austria joined France – this was enough to keep both Russia and Austria neutral. Denmark toyed with the idea of supporting France in the hope of recovering Schleswig from Prussia, but in the end did nothing, while Italy made such outrageous demands on France as the price of her support, that Napoleon would not accept them. Britain was not prepared to intervene in a war that did not appear to affect her interests. She was certainly unwilling to come to France's assistance, particularly after Bismarck made it appear as if Napoleon was about to invade Belgium in defiance of the longstanding British guarantee of Belgian independence. He did this by publishing in *The Times* an undated version of draft documents given to him by the French ambassador in 1867, when they were discussing possible 'compensation' for French neutrality during the Seven Weeks' War. These documents mentioned Belgium specifically, and Bismarck appears to have kept them carefully for use in just such circumstances as arose in July 1870.

* The Prussian army, with troops from the other German states, was quickly mobilized. Mobilization had been well planned, and nearly half a million troops had been moved by train into the Rhineland, on the borders of Alsace, by the beginning of August. The soldiers were generally well trained, and they were under the command of the brilliant General von Moltke. French mobilization began in the middle of July but was slower and not complete by the time Napoleon III arrived at Metz to take supreme command at the end of the month.

The first battles of the war took place at the beginning of August. The French troops had the advantage of the new *chasse-pot* rifles and elementary machine guns, the *mitrailleuses*, but the fire power of the Prussian artillery proved decisive.

These early German victories had a catastrophic effect on Napoleon. He went on the defensive, withdrawing 180 000 men into the fortress of Metz. There would be no French invasion of Germany. The only question was how long it would be before a German invasion of France began. It came a week later on 14 August, when the German armies crossed the River Moselle at several points and advanced beyond Metz to cut off the French escape route to Paris. Two days later the French army in Metz attempted to withdraw to the north, but was defeated in a fierce battle and forced to retreat into the fortress again. There it remained besieged until it finally surrendered at the end of October. The decision to remain in Metz was fatal to the French cause for it meant that the bulk of Napoleon's finest troops were out of action.

Napoleon had left Metz when the fighting began, and reached the River Marne, where a new French army was hurriedly collected together under the command of MacMahon. MacMahon set off with 130 000 men to find and rescue the army which was supposed to be breaking out of Metz in the direction of Sedan. In fact Metz was besieged by half the German army and the half-hearted attempt to break out was unsuccessful. The other half of the German army intercepted MacMahon's forces and drove them back in confusion towards Sedan, near the Belgian border.

On 1 September the most important battle of the war began, watched from a hill top by William I, Moltke, Bismarck and a selection of German princes. The French commander refused to consider a retreat despite the severe battering his troops were receiving. 'We *must* have a victory', he said. It was a forlorn hope. Eventually he was compelled to order a retreat. Napolean rode round during the battle, looking hopefully for a bullet which would spare him the disgrace of surrender. He did not find one.

* That night Bismarck, Moltke and the French commander met to discuss surrender terms. In a letter to his wife Bismarck described what happened next:

1 Yesterday at five o'clock in the morning, after I had been discussing until one o'clock in the morning with Moltke and the French generals the terms of the capitulation, General Reille woke me to tell me that Napoleon wished to speak with me. I rode
5 without washing and with no breakfast towards Sedan, and found the Emperor in an open carriage, with six officers, on the high road near Sedan. I dismounted, greeted him as politely as if we were in the Palace of the Tuileries in Paris and asked what were His Majesty's commands. On Napoleon's asking where he should go, I
10 offered him my quarters at Donchéry near Sedan. . . . Before we reached the place he began to be apprehensive that we might meet a number of people, and asked whether we could stop at a lonely labourer's cottage by the road. It was miserable and dirty, but 'No matter' said Napoleon; and I ascended with him a narrow ricketty
15 staircase. In a room three metres square, with a deal table and two rush bottomed chairs, we sat an hour while the others remained below – a contrast to our last interview. . . . We sent out one of the officers to reconnoitre and he discovered a little villa a kilometre away in Frenois. There I accompanied the Emperor and there we
20 concluded with the French General the capitulation, according to

Napoleon III and Bismarck on the morning after Sedan

which forty to sixty thousand French – I cannot be more accurate at this time – with all that they had, became our prisoners. The day before yesterday and yesterday [1 and 2 September 1870] cost France one hundred thousand men and an emperor. . . . This has
25 been an event of vast historic importance.

Thus ended the final meeting between Bismarck and Napoleon in a situation which neither of them could have foreseen in 1855 when they met in Paris.

The day after the battle, under the terms of surrender agreed in the early morning, the Germans took prisoner 84 000 men, 2 700 officers, 39 generals and one emperor. Later additions brought the total number of prisoners to over 104 000. Napoleon was taken to Cassel, where he remained until the spring of 1872, before going into exile in England, where he died the following year. When the news of the defeat and of the Emperor's capture reached Paris on 4 September, he was deposed by a revolutionary government. The Second Empire was abolished and the Third French Republic was proclaimed in its place.

* The war should by rights have finished at this point. There were few French troops available to continue the fighting, for most of them had either surrendered at Sedan or were still besieged in the fortress of Metz. Little stood in the way of a German advance on Paris. To everyone's surprise the war was to last for another six months.

The German forces had surrounded Paris by the middle of September, and settled down to starve the city into surrender. The government of the new French Republic struggled to raise an army in the south of France to relieve the siege of Paris, but although there was no difficulty in finding soldiers for the army, it was impossible to find enough trained men to act as officers. The result was a large, undisciplined, enthusiastically patriotic mob, which was quickly defeated by the German army.

Eventually Paris became very short of food and the government was forced to surrender. An armistice was signed on 28 January 1871. Ten days before, the King of Prussia had been proclaimed Kaiser, or German Emperor, not in Berlin but in the great French palace of Versailles just outside Paris. This was a bitter pill for the French to swallow, and added to the humiliation of the surrender.

* France was further humiliated by the terms of the peace treaty, signed at Frankfurt in May 1871. German troops were to remain in eastern France until a heavy fine of £200 million had been paid, and Alsace and the eastern half of Lorraine were annexed to Germany. These harsh terms caused consternation in France. The Mayor of Strasburg, in Alsace, died of shock on hearing them, and in the next few years many of the inhabitants of Alsace-Lorraine emigrated to the French African colony of Algeria.

Why did Bismarck impose such a humiliating treaty on France, so different from the one which ended the Seven Weeks' War with Austria?

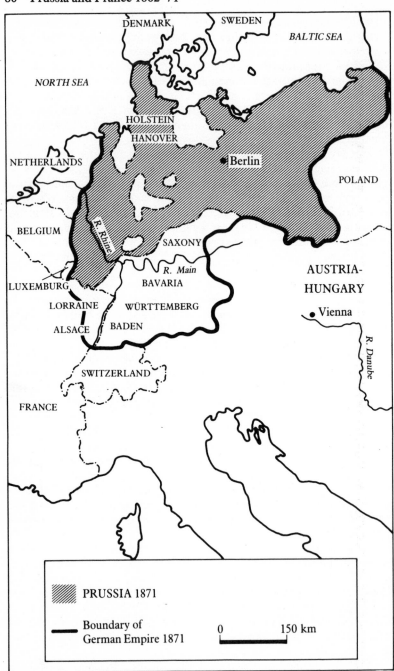

Prussia and the German Empire, 1871

Alsace and Lorraine were rich in iron ore and good agricultural land, but Bismarck's interest in them was not economic. Although a good case could be made for including Alsace in the German Reich, for Strasburg had been an Imperial City in the days of the old Holy Roman Empire, Lorraine was very French and it might have been better left unannexed. But there were good strategic reasons for taking both. Bismarck argued that Germany needed a frontier which would make a French attack impossible, and this could only be done by taking over the area around the fortresses of Metz and Strasburg beside the Rhine. Such an arrangement would also make a German attack on France easier, but he dismissed the idea, at least in public. 'In twenty wars we have never been the aggressors against France, and we claim nothing from her but the security she has so often threatened'. These proposals for making Alsace and Lorraine into buffer states let him pose as the protector of the south German states against irresponsible violence from France. It was a useful argument in winning support in the south just at the critical moment when German unity was becoming a real possibility. The war against 'the wicked French' was a useful means of speeding up unification, and government propaganda had painted Napoleon III in the blackest possible colours. France was guilty, had been justly defeated and now needed to be punished. One way of doing this was to annexe territory, and 'geographical considerations' dictated that Alsace-Lorraine should be the territory chosen.

The years 1870 and 1871 were dramatic for Bismarck and Europe, with France defeated, Germany united as an Empire, the balance of power in Europe totally altered and the beginning of a Franco-German enmity which was to last until 1945.

Making notes on *'Prussia and France 1862–71'*

This chapter is concerned with the relationship between Bismarck and Napoleon III as much as between Prussia and France. It covers Bismarck's progress towards the unification of Germany in this period during which he first used Napoleon and then destroyed him.

The following headings and subheadings should help you:

1. War with Austria
1.1. Napoleon III and Bismarck
1.2. Biarritz
1.3. Preparations for war
1.4. The Seven Weeks' War
1.5. The Treaty of Prague
2. The Luxemburg Crisis
2.1. Bismarck's policy
2.2. Diplomatic solution
3. War with France

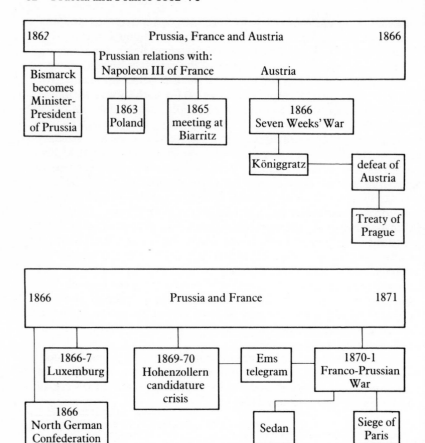

Summary – Prussia and France, 1862–71

3.1. Hohenzollern candidature crisis
3.2. The Ems Telegram
3.3. How far was the telegram the cause of war?
3.4. Declaration of war
3.5. The Franco-Prussian War
3.6. The fighting
3.7. Surrender of Napoleon III
3.8. Siege of Paris
3.9. Peace of Frankfurt

Answering essay questions on 'Prussia and France 1862–71'

The chances are that you will use evidence from this chapter and the previous one to answer specific questions about Bismarck and the unification of Germany.

Four typical examples of such questions are:

> How much did Bismarck's success from 1862 to 1870 depend on the errors and misjudgements of others? (London, 1979)
> How far was the unification of Germany achieved between 1862 and 1871 due to Bismarck's diplomacy? (JMB)
> Assess Bismarck's contribution to German unification (Scottish, 1983)
> What did the foundation of the German Empire owe to Bismarck? (Oxford and Cambridge, 1980)

All these questions are of the same basic type. They require you to construct a two part answer. One part argues, 'Yes . . . in these ways/to this extent'. The other part argues, 'No . . . in these ways/to this extent'.

Look at the first question. In this case the approach would be, 'Yes Bismarck's success was largely/to some extent due to the errors of others because . . ., *but* other factors were also important, such as . . .'. Draw up an essay plan for this question.

Make a list of reasons to support the argument that Bismarck's success was due to the errors of others. Then make a second list, this time of the other factors involved in what you consider their order of importance, with supporting statements.

Source-based questions on 'Prussia and France, 1862–71'

1 Bismarck's interview with a British journalist
Read carefully the report of Bismarck's statement, given on pages 69–70. Answer the following questions:
a) What is the point that Bismarck devoted most of the interview to communicating?
b) There are at least three other significant points that Bismarck 'slipped in'. What are they?
c) Summarize Bismarck's 'message' in giving the interview. Include the points you have identified in a) and b), as well as your interpretation of Bismarck's motive for wanting these points reported in Britain.
d) What reasons would an historian give for refusing to take Bismarck's words, quoted in the interview, at face value?

2 The Ems Telegram
Read carefully the extracts from Bismarck's *Reminiscences* describing

what happened to the Ems Telegram, given on pages 73–4, and the translation of the telegram, given on page 73. Answer the following questions:

a) Why were Generals von Roon and von Moltke 'so depressed' by the contents of the original telegram? Support your answer with evidence.

b) What was the significance of Bismarck's editing of the Ems Telegram? Support your answer with evidence.

c) Bismarck implies his reasons for acting as he did. What were these reasons? Support your answer with evidence.

d) What aspects of Bismarck's account in his *Reminiscences* are most open to challenge? Explain your answer.

3 The declaration of war, July 1870

Read carefully the extract from the French declaration of war, given on page 75, and the extract from Bismarck's memorandum, given on page 75. Answer the following questions:

a) In what ways was the French case for declaring war unconvincing?

b) What were Bismarck's motives in issuing his memorandum? Support your answer with evidence.

4 The Surrender of Napoleon III, September 1870

Read carefully the extract from Bismarck's letter to his wife, given on pages 77–9, and study the illustration on page 80. Answer the following questions:

a) What conclusions can be drawn from Bismarck's evidence about Napoleon's state of mind? Support your answer with evidence.

b) What, apart from providing a factual account of what happened, appear to have been Bismarck's motives in writing his letter? Support your answer with evidence.

c) The painting reproduced on page 78 was not an attempt to make a visual record of what actually happened. It was painted with other purposes in mind. Using evidence from the painting, suggest what these other purposes might have been.

d) In what ways do the letter and the painting i) support, and ii) contradict each other?

CHAPTER 5

Bismarck's Germany 1870–90

1 The German Empire

January 18, 1871 began as a triumphal day for Bismarck. In the Hall of Mirrors, in the great palace of Versailles outside Paris, King William I of Prussia was proclaimed Emperor of a united Germany. The Franco-Prussian War was in its final stages. Ten days later Paris surrendered and the German victory was assured. In the meantime, the fact that the ceremony was taking place in Versailles, the palace built by the greatest of the French Kings, Louis XIV, marked the defeat of France even before the surrender.

Soon after midday the King of Prussia entered the Hall. A short religious service was held, enlivened by a fiery sermon directed against the French. After a brief speech of welcome by the King, Bismarck, in splended array in his pale blue military uniform, stepped forward to read the proclamation:

1 We William, by the Grace of God, King of Prussia, and after the German princes and free cities have unanimously appealed to us to renew the Imperial dignity, which has been in abeyance for more than sixty years [since 1806 and the end of the Holy Roman
5 Empire] . . . hereby inform you that we regard it as our duty to the whole Fatherland to respond to this summons of the allied German princes and free cities and assume the German imperial title. May God grant to us and to our successors to the Imperial crown that we may be defenders of the German Empire at all times, not in military
10 conquests, but in the works of peace, in the sphere of national prosperity, freedom and civilisation.

After these praiseworthy sentiments, the ceremony continued despite a little difficulty about the title. William had set his heart on 'Kaiser (Emperor) of Germany', but as part of a deal made with the King of Bavaria to gain his support, Bismarck had agreed that the title should be 'German Kaiser'. The situation was saved by the Grand Duke of Baden, William's son-in-law, who neatly got round the problem by shouting out 'Long live his Imperial and Royal Majesty, Kaiser William'. William was not amused. Gravely displeased, he pointedly ignored Bismarck as the royal party left the platform.

Bismarck could afford to disregard William's displeasure, for he had achieved his aim. He had been determined that William should not feel it necessary to refuse the imperial crown as Frederick William had done in 1849. William was known to be reluctant to accept a 'German' title, which would take precedence over his Prussian one, and so careful preparations were needed. The offer of the Imperial crown had to come from the Princes, not from the German people, as it had done in 1849.

In October 1870 Bismarck had begun his negotiations. Ludwig II, King of Bavaria, who, as a result of his insatiable building mania, was heavily in debt, was easily persuaded, by a financial offer he could not refuse, to put his name to a letter asking William to accept the title of Emperor. Other princes were then persuaded to add their names, and the document was sent to William. The appeal was seconded in December, 1870, by a deputation to William from the North German *Reichstag*. Strangely enough the President of the *Reichstag* in 1870 was the same man who had been spokesman for the Frankfurt Assembly when it offered the imperial crown to Frederick William in 1849. This time, though, the Parliament had only a subsidiary role to play and was merely a backing group for the Princes.

a) *The Constitution*

The new German Empire, of which William was Kaiser, was a federal state now reduced from the 39 states of the German Confederation to 25 by the loss of Austria and by the Prussian annexations. In due course were added Alsace and Lorraine newly acquired from France at the end of the war. It was an amalgam of the North German Confederation, including Prussia, with the south German states. It was a mixture of territories each of which had its own traditions. The main problem was to unite them in fact as well as in theory.

The aim of the liberals of 1849 to create a German national state now appeared to have been achieved, although not in a manner they would have approved. Their aim had been a Germany united by a popular national movement; the reality was a unity imposed from above, a Prussian dominated Empire, brought into being by Bismarck.

The constitution of the new Empire was based directly on that of the North German Confederation (see pages 60–1), although the Kaiser could not declare war without the agreement of the *Bundesrat* unless Germany were attacked. Prussia, as the largest state, dominated the *Bundesrat* with 17 out of 58 votes. Only 14 votes were needed to block any proposals to alter the constitution, which meant Prussia could always veto any changes if she wished to do so. Other decisions were reached by a majority vote, but in practice, with nearly 30 per cent of the votes, Prussia was never outvoted. In the *Reichstag*, Prussia had a majority of representatives, and with the King of Prussia as Kaiser, and Bismarck as Imperial Chancellor, Prussia's predominance was assured. From 1871 to 1890 Bismarck remained as Chancellor and all decisions of state were made by him, often forcing the elderly Kaiser to agree to actions against his inclinations.

The whole constitution with its involved relationships between Emperor, Chancellor, ministers, *Bundesrat*, *Reichstag*, the individual states and their rulers, and the people gave very little opportunity for the exercise of democracy, and was further complicated by the elevated status of the army. The army had been a very important, indeed the central, element in Prussian life since the time of Frederick the Great in the previous century. In the 1870s and 1880s it was still taken for granted that the army's needs must always come first and that the highest virtues were military ones. Uniforms brought exaggerated respect and obedience; both Bismarck and the Kaiser always wore uniform in public. The Kaiser at least had the excuse that he was Commander-in-Chief of the Imperial forces as well as those of Prussia. Prussian military influence rapidly extended throughout the rest of Germany after 1870 and even in Bavaria, where the King kept his right to command his own troops in peace time, the army was increasingly officered by Prussians. Because of the importance of the army the Generals had enormous influence on government policy, and because the military budget was not subject to annual approval by the *Reichstag*, they were independent of continued Parliamentary control.

* In the days of the North German Confederation, Bismarck had struggled with the *Reichstag* over who should control the amount of military spending. A compromise had been reached in 1867, between Bismarck and the liberal opposition which agreed that the so-called 'Iron', or military, budget should remain at a fixed level but outside the control of the *Reichstag* until 1 January 1872. After that the budget would be reviewed. The numbers of new recruits to the army, which was what governed the amount of money needed, would be fixed by law and the *Reichstag* would need to give approval. During the Franco-Prussian War it had been agreed to extend the fixed 1867 budget until 1874, when the problem surfaced again.

The National Liberals, now the majority party, defended the right of the *Reichstag* to control military spending. Bismarck threatened the National Liberals and accused them of trying to undermine German military strength. In the end a further compromise was reached. The military budget was to be fixed for seven years at a time, rather than voted on annually or fixed permanently.

* This situation was a grave disappointment to the Liberals but appears to have been perfectly acceptable and reasonable to the majority of the German people. There was no strong feeling that government should be in the hands of the political party which happened to have a majority of seats in the *Reichstag*, instead of being left to the Chancellor and ministers. There was strong support for the idea that it was right and proper that the Emperor (or his Chancellor) should rule. Even members of the more extreme left-wing parties did not expect the *Reichstag* to exercise much control over government, and they certainly did not expect it to take over. The most they hoped for was that it would have some influence on government decisions. Without help from the Chancellor there was little chance that the *Reichstag* would develop into a democratic, parliamentary form of government, and there was little hope

of any help from Bismarck. He saw the *Reichstag* as a collection of squabbling politicians, who did not reflect popular opinion. Even if they did, he would still have regarded them as unimportant. It was inevitable that he should clash with the National Liberal and Centre Parties over the amount of direct influence which the *Reichstag* should have in government.

2 Domestic Policies

In the early 1870s Bismarck relied for support in the *Reichstag* on the National Liberals, who were the largest single party. As he became more firmly established as Chancellor his views changed. He became more confident and began to look down on them and to treat them as his servants. He could do this because his position was strong. The Kaiser had come to regard him as indispensable; governmental ministers and the civil service were under his control and carried out his orders.

The first few years of the new Empire came to be known as the *Gründungszeit*, 'the foundation time'. The economy was booming and Bismarck and the National Liberals together pushed through legislation on economic and legal matters. These involved the introduction of nationwide systems of currency and weights and measures as well as the encouragement of common standards in banking and the completion of a national network of railways. These were seen by Bismarck and the National Liberals to be vital steps along the road of changing the hastily imposed political unification into a real national unity. To this end it was necessary to replace local or regional ways of doing things with a national system.

* After the quarrel over the military budget had been patched up in 1874, the national Liberals continued to irritate Bismarck with what he considered their unreasonable insistence on parliamentary rights. In 1877 Bismarck's chance came. The National Liberals suffered considerable losses in the election and found themselves with only a small majority in the *Reichstag*. Industrialists and landowners had both been demanding the introduction of tariffs (import duties on foreign goods) to protect home industries and produce. Bismarck had followed a policy of free trade up to this time as part of his alliance with the National Liberals, who were opposed to any kind of protection. Suddenly, he changed his policy. As usual he had a number of reasons for doing so.

Firstly, by introducing tariffs he would gain support not only from industrialists and landowners, but also from the Conservative and Centre Parties in the *Reichstag*. Both these parties were in favour of protecting home industry, and they were large enough to allow him to ignore the opposition of the National Liberals.

In addition, Bismarck saw financial advantage. One of the difficulties the federal government had was its financial instability, due, at least in part, to the fact that it was not able to raise money by direct taxation, such as income tax, but rather had to rely on indirect taxation, such as customs and excise. This left a deficit, because indirect taxation did not raise enough money for the needs of the federal government, and the balance had to be made up by what were called 'matricular' payments made by the individual states, calculated on the basis of their populations. If tariffs were introduced they would be agreed by the *Reichstag* for several years at a time, and would provide a valuable fixed income and a more stable financial base for the government.

Bismarck, as Chancellor, addressed the *Reichstag* on 2 May 1879.

1 The only country [which persists in a policy of free trade] is England, and that will not last long. France and America have departed completely from this line; Austria instead of lowering her tariffs has made them higher; Russia has done the same. . . .
5 Therefore to be alone the dupe of an honourable conviction cannot be expected from Germany for ever. By opening wide the doors of our state to the imports of foreign countries, we have become the dumping ground for the production of those countries. . . . Since we have become swamped by the surplus production of foreign
10 nations, our prices have been depressed; and the development of our industries and our entire economic position has suffered in consequence.
    Let us finally close our doors and erect some barriers, as we have proposed to you, in order to reserve for German industries at least
15 the home market, which because of German good nature, has been exploited by foreigners. The problem of a large export trade is always a very delicate one; there are no new lands to discover, the world has been circumnavigated, and we can no longer find abroad new purchasers of importance to whom we can send our
20 goods. . . .
    I see that those countries which have adopted protection are prospering, and that those countries which have free trade are deteriorating.

In a vote the National Liberals were defeated by the protectionist Conservative and Centre parties and in July 1879 tariffs were imposed on imported agricultural and manufactured goods. The alliance with the National Liberals had ended and a new political pattern had emerged. In the process an opportunity had been taken by Bismarck to stress national interests and to further strengthen the identity of feeling among Germans by stressing the ways in which other countries were acting against Germany in economic interests.

b) *The Kulturkampf*

Bismarck's aim in his domestic policy was always to unify and consolidate the new *Reich* (Empire) socially and politically. He was suspicious of minorities, which might threaten the Protestant, Prussianized government he had so carefully set up, and he saw plots and subversive activities everywhere. Chief among his enemies he believed were the Catholics. Later their place was taken by the Socialists. In his somewhat distorted view both groups were agents of international forces, pledged to the destruction of Prussian influence in Germany, and to be dealt with accordingly. The Catholics, in particular, were thought by Bismarck to typify the groups who most resented the expansion of Prussian power. They were numerous among the racial minorities – the French in the West and the Poles in the east – who had no wish to be within the German *Reich*; in the south German states which still tended to identify with Austria rather than with Prussia; and even in the Rhinelands where, although Prussian since 1815, the people retained considerable resentment at the way they were despised by 'the Prussians'. To attack the Catholics seemed to Bismarck an ideal way of weakening one of the major causes of national disunity.

In 1871 Bismarck came into conflict with the Roman Catholic Church in a struggle known as the *Kulturkampf*. It is not easy to translate this German word. It is usually given as 'struggle for culture' or 'struggle of civilisation'. It really means the struggle for power between two very different religions and political ways of life. Much of Prussia and most of the north German states were Protestant, while the Rhine states and the states in the south were Catholic. The North German Confederation had therefore been largely Protestant, but the formation of the Empire meant that the North German Protestants were joined with a large number of Catholics. Nevertheless, the Catholics were still in a minority. Early in 1871, in order to protect themselves and their church they formed a political party called the Centre Party. They stood for religious freedom for the individual and also believed that the state should protect the rights of its citizens and should be concerned with social conditions, especially among the poor.

In the elections for the new *Reichstag* in the same year the Centre Party won 57 seats. Bismarck saw this success for the Centre Party as a very grave danger to the unity of the new Empire. He thought that the Party would encourage civil disobedience among Catholics whenever the policies of the state conflicted with those of the Pope. He decided to take action and was helped in this by a division among the Catholics themselves.

In 1870 the Pope found himself in increasing difficulties with the seizure by Italian troops of the remaining Papal lands confining him to the Vatican, and a general weakening of his control over the Roman Catholic Church everywhere. One way in which he tried to strengthen his position was by issuing a proclamation that any official statement made by the Pope about faith or morals could not be wrong, and must be accepted by all Catholics. This was called the doctrine of 'Papal Infallibility'. It meant that Catholics could face difficult choices between the demands of their church and their country.

* Some German Catholics refused to accept the new doctrine of Papal Infallibility. There were only about 5000 of these 'Old Catholics', a small minority in the Church, but Bismarck saw them as a useful ally against the rest of the Catholic Church in general, and against the Centre Party in particular. He decided to give them state support. When 'Old Catholic' teachers and professors were dismissed from schools and universities by Catholic bishops, Bismarck had an excuse to attack the Catholic Church.

As usual, he proceeded with great thoroughness. His anti-Catholic campaign began with a series of violent newspaper articles. Although it was centred in Prussia and directed against the Catholics of the Prussian Rhineland and Poland, the effects were felt throughout the Empire. In 1871 the Catholic section of the Prussian Ministry of Religion and Education was abolished and the following year Catholic rights to supervize Catholic schools were withdrawn. The Jesuits, the religious order of the Society of Jesus, whose members had always been great missionaries, teachers and supporters of Papal authority, were expelled from the whole Empire. Even German-born Jesuits were sent into exile for how could they be loyal both to the Pope and to Germany?

* In May 1873 came the climax of the campaign, when the Falk Laws, sometimes called the 'May Laws', were passed. Dr Falk was the Prussian Minister of Religion and Education and his laws brought the Catholic Church much more closely under state control. Catholic education came under state supervision, including the education of priests themselves. Only those who had studied in Germany and passed a state examination could become priests. The appointments of clergy were to be made by the state, and a civil marriage service was made compulsory, first in Prussia and then in the rest of the Empire. This meant that although couples could have a church wedding if they wanted to, the legal basis of the marriage was the state ceremony performed by state officials. Having got rid of the Jesuits, all other religious orders, except nursing orders, were dissolved, state financial aid to the Catholic Church was ended, and Prussian Catholics were deprived of legal and civil rights.

* Much to Bismarck's anger, this campaign had the opposite effect to that intended. It strengthened Catholic morale and determination, so that in the 1874 elections the Centre Party increased the number of seats it held in the *Reichstag* to 91 . Even worse, a young Catholic had the temerity to try to assassinate Bismarck. The Pope, Pius IX, now an old man but still full of fight, sent a letter to all German bishops instructing them to disobey the anti-Catholic Laws. Bismarck forbade the bishops to publish the Pope's letter. It was stalemate.

This unsatisfactory state of affairs continued until 1878, when the death of Pope Pius IX and the election of a new Pope gave Bismarck the chance to escape from what even he recognized as an impossible situation. He had underestimated the enemy, for the Catholic Church had greater strength and more popular support than he had bargained for, and the persecution of the previous seven years had only increased it. Worries about international plots against Germany masterminded by the Catholic Church had proved groundless. Even Bismarck admitted that there was now no reason for attacking Catholics in Germany, if indeed there ever had been. He had kept the support of the National Liberals because they believed that he was fighting for progress against the medieval powers of the Catholic Church, although they could not approve of the repressive way he was doing it. But many Protestant groups were now becoming anxious about the extension of state control over religion and education, and the whittling away of individual rights.

The *Kulturkampf* had been a failure. It had increased disunity, not removed it. Bismarck needed to bring it to an end, but he wanted a face-saving way of doing it, and with as little trouble to himself as possible. He began by putting all the blame for the May Laws on Dr Falk. Dr Falk resigned, and in 1880 the repeal of the May Laws began. Not all the Laws were repealed; civil marriages continued and the Jesuits were not allowed back into Germany. The new Pope was conciliatory and direct negotiations led to an improved relationship between Bismarck and the Catholic Church after 1878.

This was just the time when Bismarck was falling out with his old friends, the National Liberals, over tariffs. In a complete change of direction he now joined forces with his old enemies, the Centre Party, against his new enemies, the Socialists, Yet no one publicly questioned his actions or his suitability to continue as Chancellor. He had the continued support of the Kaiser, firm control over the administration and his hold on power remained as secure as ever, although within a single year he had abandoned the Liberals and Free Trade and adopted Protection, he had abandoned his anti-Catholic campaign, and allied himself with the Catholic Centre Party, and he had embarked on a new political witchhunt against the socialists. Thus Bismarck's religious and political policies all changed in 1878-9.

b) *The Socialists*

The Socialists were an obvious target for Bismarck's attack. They were anti-monarchist revolutionaries. At least that was the line taken in their official policy statements. In fact they were generally much milder and less revolutionary than they liked to appear. The Universal German Workingmen's Association had been formed in Prussia in 1863 as a moderate organization to help workers obtain more political power by peaceful means. Soon it fell into the hands of Marxists and became rather more extreme in its views. In 1875 it amalgamated with a second organization, the Social Democratic Labour Party. Members of the combined party became the Social Democrats.

Bismarck became increasingly alarmed as Socialists gained seats in the *Reichstag*, two in 1871, nine in 1874, 12 in 1877. Like Catholicism, socialism was international, its members who came from many different countries, were united in furthering socialist ideals and policies, even where these conflicted with national loyalties. Bismarck again began seeing plots against Germany from outside the Empire, and disunity and subversion from within. How could one be loyal both to an international organization and to one's own country? Again, as in his conflict with the Catholics, he misjudged the situation. But this time he overestimated, not underestimated the enemy; the Socialists were not as strong nor as revolutionary as he believed. He was out of sympathy with their aims and regarded them as little better than thieves and murderers, a threat to society and especially to landowners like himself. The Commune in Paris in 1871 confirmed his worst fears about socialists and revolution. A largely working class revolutionary Committee took over the city with the support of most Parisians. Control was re-established by the government only after a short but savage civil war.

The Social Democrat Party in Germany held a conference in 1875 and drew up a programme calling for the nationalization of banks, coal-mines and industry, and for social equality. Bismarck was not prepared to allow these ideas to spread and in 1876 he introduced a Bill into the *Reichstag* to control the press and prevent the publication of socialist propaganda. The Bill was defeated. The Socialists continued to gain ground and the following year nearly half a million Germans voted for them in the election.

* In 1878 there were two assassination attempts against the Kaiser. In the first a plumber fired shots at the 81-year-old monarch in Berlin. Bismarck decided to blame the Socialists for the attack, and introduced an anti-Socialist Bill into the *Reichstag*. It was defeated. Less than a month later a second attempt was made to kill the Kaiser. This time the assassin wounded him quite badly. Bismarck used this second attack as a means of damaging both his current enemies, the National Liberals and the Socialists. He launched newspaper attacks on the Liberals for failing to protect the Kaiser from Socialist would-be assassins (although there was no evidence that either assassin had any connection with the Socialists) and then persuaded the Kaiser to dissolve the *Reichstag*.

As Bismarck hoped, his propaganda had been effective. The National Liberals lost 40 seats and the Conservatives gained 37. A new Anti-Socialist Bill was presented to the *Reichstag*. Bismarck persuaded the members that public morals were being undermined by the Socialists. Even if they were not directly responsible for the attacks on the Kaiser, Bismarck claimed that pernicious socialist influences had led others to the attempted murders. Therefore, he argued, the Socialist Party, should be suppressed, in order to purify German life and to remove a major source of disloyalty. The *Reichstag* was doubtful about the logic of this argument, but eventually the Bill was passed in October 1878, because the National Liberals, afraid that Bismarck would call yet another election, did not vote against it. All socialist clubs and meetings were prohibited, and socialist publications banned. Agitators could be sent into exile and other Socialists could be imprisoned or forcibly removed from their homes to remote parts of Germany. Police powers were enormously increased.

The law had the same effect on the Socialists as the May Laws had had on the Catholics: it united them, and their support in the country increased. About 1500 Socialists were imprisoned and a great many emigrated, mostly to the United States. But the Socialist vote nearly doubled between 1878 and 1887 to over three quarters of a million, although the Anti-Socialist Act remained in force until Bismarck's dismissal in 1890. Bismarck had failed again. Repression was not working and the minority groups of Catholics and Socialists, which he suspected of threatening the Lutheran, monarchist Prussian *Kleindeutschland*, continued to thrive. The 'Enemies of the *Reich*' would not be suppressed. He turned to other and more subtle means. The stick had failed – perhaps the carrot would succeed.

* A series of paternalistic laws was proposed by which the state would improve the condition of the workers, by what Bismarck called a system of State Socialism. This was designed to take the initiative away from the Social Democrats. He expected that the workers would then turn with loyal gratitude and devotion to the State as the only source of their welfare, and that the unity of the people would be safeguarded. As a bonus, Bismarck expected that the workers, their social and economic needs satisfied, would give up what he considered to be their altogether unreasonable demands for political power.

In a speech to the *Reichstag* in 1881 he convinced the Conservative and Centre Parties, who were now in a majority, that they should accept his proposals. He played on their fears of the Social Democrats, and suggested that control over the people could be best maintained by a limited state welfare system.

1 A beginning must be made with the task of reconciling the labouring classes with the state. A remedy cannot be sought only through the repression of socialist excesses. It is necessary to have a definite advancement in the welfare of the working classes. The
5 matter of first importance is the care of those workers who are incapable of earning a living. Previous provision for guarding workers against the risk of falling into helplessness through incapacity caused by accident or age have not proved adequate, and the inadequacy of such provisions has been a main contributing
10 cause driving the working classes to seek help by joining the Social Democratic movement. Whoever has a pension assured to him for his old age is more contented and easier to manage than a man who has none.

In 1883 the first of his proposals for State Socialism became law. The Sickness Insurance Act provided medical treatment and up to 13 weeks' sick pay to three million low-paid workers and their families. The workers paid two-thirds of the contribution and the employers one-third. A worker who was permanently disabled or sick for more than 13 weeks was given protection by the Accident Insurance Act of 1884. The cost of this was met by the employers. In 1886 it was extended to cover seven million agricultural workers. Finally in 1889 came the Old Age and Disability Act which gave pensions to those over 70, and disablement pensions for those who were younger. The cost of the scheme was divided between the workers, the employers and the state, all of whom contributed to it.

   * The scheme was a very remarkable one. It was the first of its kind in the world and was much more extensive than might have been expected at the time. Its reception at first was mixed. It was well received by some workers, although others thought it was 'a sham' particularly as the government was still opposing the formation of Trade Unions, and could not therefore have the workers' interests at heart. At the same time employers grumbled at the trouble and expense of 'sticking in eleven million stamps every Saturday evening', especially as most of them could see no advantage to themselves in the scheme.

   Historians have argued about Bismarck's motives for the introduction of State Socialism. He may have been acting on purely humanitarian principles, but this seems unlikely. He may have been trying to cut the ground from beneath the feet of the Socialists or perhaps to make a political bid for the support of the workers, both of which are possibilities. Much the most likely is the argument he himself put forward that the scheme would make the German people 'more contented and easier to manage'. And, for a time at least, they were.

3 Foreign Policy

The German victory of 1870 altered the balance of power in Europe. The German Empire which resulted with its large population, great economic potential and strong army, was clearly going to be a new and important element in international relations. It would take time, though, to establish the Empire firmly and external security would be vital to Germany over the next few years.

   The great danger was likely to come from the government of the new French Republic, which was still smarting under the loss of Alsace-Lorraine at the end of the war. The best way of reducing this threat, Bismarck believed, was to isolate France by ensuring that all the Great Powers, except France, needed Germany's support and were 'prevented as far as possible from forming coalitions against us by virtue of their relations to one another.'

   He manipulated what has been called the 'balance of tensions' among the Powers to ensure that it remained favourable to Germany. Countries anxious for war should be encouraged to fight each other and so leave

Germany at peace. At the very least they should be kept in a state of mutual suspicion, if not in armed conflict. At the same time he pursued a system of alliances aimed at preserving German security. He believed that safety lay in 'trying to be one of three as long as the world is governed by the unstable equilibrium of five great powers' (Britain, France, Russia, Austria-Hungary and Germany). If he could achieve this Germany would always be in a position of advantage whether in diplomatic negotiations or in war. His main fear was of a coalition of France, Russia and Austria-Hungary against him. He therefore attempted to be on good terms with both Russia and Austria-Hungary. This he was largely successful in doing despite the fact that the two Powers almost came to blows on several occasions over the declining Ottoman Empire in the Balkans.

Bismarck's foreign policy in the 1870s and 1880s was largely defensive. He was mainly concerned with giving the new German Empire that he had played a large part in creating a breathing space during which real unity could be developed following unification. (International affairs between 1870 and 1914 are discussed at length in another volume in this series.)

4 Bismarck's Departure

While the Emperor William I lived, Bismarck's hold on power was never in question. Their meetings were often stormy, emotional and noisy. They shouted, threw things, burst into tears and quarrelled for much of the time. But they understood each other. 'It is not easy to be the Emperor under such a Chancellor' William remarked, but he managed it successfully, mainly by letting Bismarck have his own way.

When William died in March 1888 he was succeeded briefly by his son Frederick, who died from cancer only three months later. The imperial crown then passed to Frederick's son, William II. He was a convinced German nationalist and was totally committed to the belief that he ruled by Divine Right. 'Remember the German people are chosen by God. On me as the German Emperor, the spirit of God has descended. I am his weapon, his sword, his vice regent'. Intelligent, talented, and cultured, William was in sharp contrast to his grandfather, the straightforward military man. While he too was a soldier, 'We belong to each other – I and the army – we were born for each other', the young Emperor's character was far from simple or straightforward. It was complex and full of contradictions. A physical deformity from birth, a near useless left arm, of which he was very conscious, seems to have contributed to his personality problems. His behaviour was erratic, at times almost unbalanced.

He was undoubtedly overbearing and arrogant; but then so was the Chancellor. They did not get on at all well. Bismarck thought William young (he was 29), and foolish, and treated him in a very condescending manner. Once again his judgement was at fault – he underestimated William.

The Emperor was determined to rule as well as to reign. 'I shall let the old man shuffle on for six months' he told friends, 'then I shall rule myself'. The 'old man' saw no need for anything to change. Open conflict was bound to come. They quarrelled over foreign policy, over Bismarck's proposal that the Anti-Socialist Laws be made permanent, and over William's suggestions for social reform. These included an end to child labour and Sunday working. When these reforms were discussed in the Crown Council in January 1890 Bismarck opposed them.

In February, the elections showed a swing to the left, with big gains for the Social Democrats and for the Progressives, another party favouring radical reform. Bismarck's support in the country was waning. In an attempt to recover his position he proposed an extraordinary scheme: the *Reichstag* would be asked to agree to a large increase in the army and a new and extremely repressive anti-Socialist law. If, as was probable, they refused, an assembly of German Princes would meet, alter the constitution and drastically curtail the powers of the *Reichstag*. The Kaiser refused to allow the plan to be put into operation. Relations between the two men became even worse.

* In March the Kaiser and Chancellor quarrelled bitterly about the right of ministers to advise the monarch. Bismarck had revived an old order first issued in 1852 by Frederick William IV, which forbade ministers to approach the King (of Prussia) except through the Minister-President. Bismarck interpreted this to mean that all ministers must obtain permission from him as Chancellor, before they could discuss any government business with the Emperor.

William was not prepared for such restrictions and commanded that the 1852 order be immediately withdrawn. He sent Bismarck an ultimatum – resign or be dismissed. Three days later Bismarck sent a long letter of justification for his actions, accusations of Imperial ingratitude – and his resignation. This letter was not made public until after his death and the official announcement merely implied that the Chancellor had resigned for health reasons. The German people were led to believe that he had offered his resignation voluntarily and that every effort by the Kaiser to persuade him to change his mind had been in vain. These bland statements brought to an end the career of the 'Iron Chancellor', 'not with a bang but a whimper'.

In a newspaper interview soon after his retirement Bismarck was quoted as saying:

1   My dismissal was not a thing of yesterday. I had seen it coming. The Emperor wished to be his own Chancellor, with no one intervening between his ministers and himself. . . . Sooner or later he will learn from experience. . . . He had ideas which I could not
5   approve. And our characters did not harmonize. The old Emperor

DROPPING THE PILOT.

Punch cartoon, 29 March, 1890

asked my opinion about everything and told me his own. The young one consulted other people and wished to decide for himself. I too wanted to go, though not just at the moment when he sent two messengers to hurry me. Matters of importance for the
10 *Reich* were in progress, and I did not wish to see my achievements of a quarter of a century scattered like chaff. Yet I am not angry with him, nor perhaps he with me.

He was right about the personality clash, but wrong about his feelings for William II. He *was* angry with the Kaiser, and retired with ill grace to write his very lengthy, confused and biased memoirs, complaining the while, to anyone who would listen, about William II and about the new Chancellor and his policies. He, the arch-monarchist, was even heard to speak in favour of a Republican form of government, for kings, he said, were dangerous if they had power. Rumour had it that after his retirement he always placed his money with the reverse side, the German eagle, uppermost, because he could not bear to look on the false face of the Kaiser. True or not, the fact that the story was told and believed shows the depth of Bismarck's feelings against William II.

After 1892 Bismarck's health began to fail and in July 1898 he died. The mausoleum being built for him and his wife, who had died four years earlier, was not ready and his coffin remained in his house until the following Spring. On 1 April 1899, on what would have been his eighty-fourth birthday, Bismarck was buried. On his grave were the words, 'A faithful German servant of Kaiser William I'.

a) *Assessment of Bismarck*

Although his body was laid to rest, Bismarck's spirit has continued to haunt German history. Historians have argued over his achievements and his reputation, his motives and his methods. For most historians the unification of Germany has meant Bismarck. Innumerable books have been written about him. By 1895, five years after his resignation, there were already 650 biographies available. Twenty years later there were 3500 and the number has gone on increasing ever since. The history of the unification of Germany is in danger of being submerged in a morass of biographical details.

When it comes to primary evidence the problem is not a lack of material but an excess, much of it conflicting. Bismarck left a wealth of letters, articles, speeches and official reports. There were also his voluminous *Reminiscences*, written long after the events and in a time of great bitterness. They are not entirely reliable, for fact was often embroidered with a little fiction.

During his time in office, he frequently made totally contradictory statements at the same time about the same events. Shortly before the outbreak of the Franco-Prussian War, for instance, in letters and conversations, he was arguing both in favour of war as a means of rapid unification, and in favour of peaceful evolution towards unification through economic means such as the *Zollverein*.

Some historians see this provision of contradictory evidence as symptomatic of Bismarck's perversity of mind, a desire to confuse or mislead friends and enemies alike; to a sense of fun, an echo of his joke-playing days as 'the mad *Junker*'; to a lack of settled purpose and the inability to think clearly and coherently in abstract terms; or, more probably, simply as a way of 'reasoning out loud', rehearsing a number of different arguments before reaching a decision. Whatever the reason, it means that Bismarck's own evidence needs to be used with caution. A single letter or speech is not necessarily a true reflection of his policies or intentions at any given time.

If it suited him he was quite prepared to deny categorically his part in events, even when, as in the Hohenzollern candidature crisis, documentary evidence existed to the contrary. This showed that despite his claim that he was not involved before July 1870, he had sent a long memorandum on the subject to William I three months earlier. For all these reasons it is extremely difficult to disentangle with any certainty Bismarck's motives, or to decide how far he planned ahead. The story that early in 1862 he outlined to Disraeli, later the British Prime Minister, his plan to defeat Austria, destroy the German Confederation and unite Germany under Prussian leadership, is often quoted as evidence of a long-term plan which he successfully carried out. However, it is equally possible to quote evidence to suggest that his plans were quite different. Whatever had been the outcome of events there would exist evidence that Bismarck had planned it that way.

But he knew as well as anyone that in political life nothing is certain: 'Politics is not in itself an exact and logical science but is the capacity to choose in each fleeting moment of the situation that which is least harmful or most opportune.' And he was the supreme opportunist, taking advantage of French blunders in 1870, for instance, to leave France no way out of declaring war, and thus appearing as the aggressor.

His policies can best be described as flexible. It seems reasonable to assume that he did have general long-term aims, involving war with Austria and the extension of Prussian power over the other German states. It also seems reasonable to assume that the timing and the exact means of achieving these aims were left to short-term decisions based on conditions at the time; for as well as being an opportunist, he was a realist, at least as far as politics were concerned.

A realistic approach to politics, *Realpolitik*, had characterized Bismarck's political career from his earliest days. In 1850 his speech in defence of Olmütz proclaimed that the only sound foundation for a great state is not idealism, but 'state egoism' (national self interest). Thirty years later his beliefs had not changed. Defending himself against critics in the *Reichstag* who accused him of sudden changes of policy he said:

1   I have always had one compass only, one lodestar by which I have
    steered: the welfare of the state. . . . When I have had time to think
    I have always acted according to the question, 'What is useful,
    advantageous and right for my Fatherland and – as long as this was
5   only Prussia – for my dynasty, and today for the German nation'.

It was not an idealistic German nationalism which inspired Bismarck
towards unification. It was a realistic appreciation of Prussian interests
which led him to the creation of a *Kleindeutsch* Empire.

   * There are, however, historians such as Böhme who take a less
Bismarck-centred view of German unification. They argue that Bismarck did not make Germany; Germany made Bismarck. They believe
that conditions, particularly economic conditions, were such in 1862 that
Bismarck was able to build on them and gain the credit for bringing
about a unification, which given time would probably have developed
naturally. They consider that 'coal and iron', not 'blood and iron' were
the Prussian power base. The existing economic ascendency was the key
to political ascendency. There is some truth in this, and it was in fact a
view shared to some extent by Bismarck himself. He appreciated the
importance and unifying influence of the *Zollverein* and the *Zollparlament*
in the years before 1870. In the years after that date he initiated the
development of new electrical and chemical industries, the exploitation
of mineral resources, and the expansion of road and rail networks. By
1890 Germany had been welded into one economic whole.

   Whatever view is taken about the 'inevitability' of German unification,
it is clear that it happened as it did and when it did largely as a result of
Bismarck's actions. He manipulated situations even if he did not create
them, and he worked hard and successfully to ensure the outcomes he
desired. It is not surprising that the old man of 75 bitterly resented the
way in which the young man of 29 seized effective control of his creation.
If Bismarck could have lived for another 20 years he would have been
distraught at the use to which the Kaiser had put his inheritance.

Making notes on 'Bismarck's Germany 1870–90'

Your notes on this chapter should give you an understanding of the
foundation of the German Empire in 1871 and Bismarck's policies over
the next two decades, particularly in domestic affairs. You should also
have the basis for a discussion on Bismarck's part in bringing about
German unification.

   The following headings and sub-headings may be helpful:
1.   The German Empire
1.1. Proclamation at Versailles
1.2. The Constitution
1.3. The Military budget

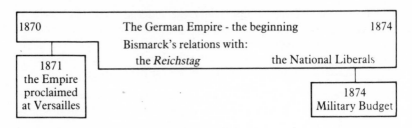

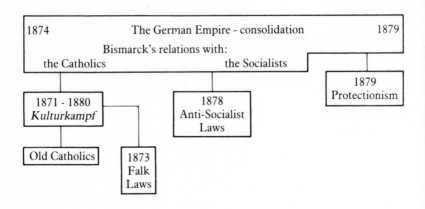

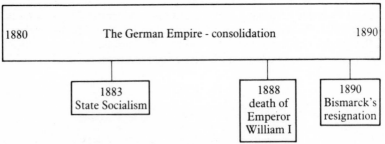

Summary – Bismarck's Germany, 1870–90

Answering essay questions on 'Bismarck's Germany, 1870–90'

Study these four questions:

> Make an appraisal of the domestic policies of Bismarck between 1871 and 1890. (WJEC, 1980)
> Examine the domestic problems facing Bismarck's Germany in the period 1871 to 1890. How successfully were they resolved? (JMB, 1981)
> Why and over what issues was there conflict between Bismarck and the *Reichstag* in the years 1871–90? (Cambridge, 1981)
> Was the *Kulturkampf* Bismarck's most serious mistake in domestic policy? (Oxford, 1982)

Make a list of the issues/topics you would need to deal with in your answer to each one. Are your four lists similar/identical? If not, why not?

Choose one of the questions. Make an essay plan for it by:

1 reading the question several times and thinking out the argument you will need to present in order to answer it.

2 writing down the key statements that summarize your argument. There must be at least two of these. Ideally there will be four or five. Each statement should encapsulate one of the major points you have to make, e.g. Bismarck misjudged the extent to which international movements threatened the unity of the German Empire.

3 assigning each of the issues/topics on the list you have already made to one or more of the key statements.

4 deciding the best order in which to deal with your key statements.

It might now be helpful to write the essay. Allow yourself only 40 minutes in which to complete it.

Source-based questions on 'Bismarck's Germany, 1870–90'

1   The Proclamation of Kaiser William, 1871
Read carefully the text of the proclamation, given on page 85. Answer the following questions:
a)   What are the implications of the 'summons' coming from the 'allied German princes and free cities'?
b)   The final sentence of the proclamation expresses sentiments that were perhaps not genuinely held. What, then, might have been the reasons for including them?

2   Bismarck and Protectionism, 1879
Read carefully the extract from Bismarck's speech to the *Reichstag*, given on page 89. Answer the following questions:
a)   Summarize in about 100 words the case in favour of abandoning free trade argued by Bismarck.
b)   What weakness in his argument does he allude to, without explaining how he intends to overcome it?
c)   What evidence does the extract contain about Bismarck's views on colonies?

3   Bismarck and State Socialism
Read carefully the extract from Bismarck's speech to the *Reichstag*, given on page 94. Answer the following questions:
a)   What argument does Bismarck use to justify his decision to press for elements of state socialism?
b)   How far are you convinced by Bismarck's argument? Support your view with evidence.
c)   What does Bismarck's choice of argument suggest about the values and attitudes of the majority in the *Reichstag*?

4   Bismarck's departure, 1890
Read carefully the extract from the newspaper article, given on pages 97–9, and study the cartoon reproduced on page 98. Answer the following questions:
a)   What does the newspaper article put forward as the main reason for Bismarck's dismissal? Justify your answer.
b)   What general impression does Bismarck appear to be attempting to give in the interview? What were likely to have been his reasons for doing this?
c)   The cartoonist is expressing a point of view. What is this? Explain your answer.
d)   In what ways do the ideas contained in the cartoon coincide with the views expressed by Bismarck in his interview?
e)   In what ways are the cartoon and the interview providing comment on different issues?

Answering essay questions about the unification of Germany in general

You should now be in a good position to think about the wider issues that lie behind what you have read in this book. You have already dealt with the specific issues. Now is the time when you need to pull all these ideas together in order to tackle questions such as:

'Favourable external and internal circumstances, not Bismarck's diplomatic genius, explain the unification of Germany.' Discuss this statement. (AEB, 1981)

'Bismarck's policy for German unification reflects the profound disillusionment engendered in Germany by the failure of the experiments of 1848.' Discuss this statement. (London, 1981)

'Nationalism was probably the most important of the causes of German unification.' Discuss. (Oxford & Cambridge, 1982)

A normal reaction when faced by questions such as these is to panic! As a result *either* the question is avoided *or* there is a temptation to write a narrative essay describing the stages of German unification from beginning to end. But with a little thought it is possible to work out what type of answer is required – and it is not a narrative.

The third question is the easiest to disentangle. Go through the following stages:

1 Decide which topic the question is about. (*German unification*)
2 Decide which aspect of the topic the question is about. (*the causes*)
3 Decide whether the question is putting forward a point of view to be agreed or disagreed with? (*Yes*)
4 Identify this point of view. (*nationalism was the most important cause*)
5 List the other points of view that should be discussed. (*nationalism was quite important; some other cause was the least important*)
6 Decide the order in which to discuss the points of view. (*nationalism most important; nationalism quite important; other cause most important*)
7 Decide how each point of view should be developed. (e.g. *it could be argued that nationalism was unimportant because of the failure of 1848 and because Bismarck and Prussian military strength were what really caused unification.*)
8 List the evidence to support each point of view you are presenting.
9 Decide what is your opinion on the issue.

Stages 1–4 involve analysing the question. There is normally only one correct answer to each stage. Stages 5–9 are a matter of judgement. There are likely to be several appropriate answers to each stage. What matters is that you clearly choose one of them and follow it through.

Try all nine stages with the first and/or second question. Write one of your answers in full.

Further Reading

Most general histories of nineteenth-century Europe do not deal in sufficient detail with German unification or with Bismarck's Germany to be particularly useful. One exception, although it does not cover the whole period, is the very readable :

J. A. S. Grenville, *Europe Reshaped 1848–1878* (Fontana 1976).

Many histories of Germany cover too wide a period of time to provide help on particular topics. The best short history is probably:

W. Carr, *A History of Germany 1815–1945* (Edward Arnold 1969).

For the period after 1866, a very well written, detailed survey is:

G. Craig, *Germany 1866–1945*, (Oxford, 1978).

There are literally hundreds of books available on Bismarck. Entertainingly written but not entirely reliable is:

A. J. P. Taylor, *Bismarck: the Man and Statesman*, (originally published 1955, reprinted 1974 by New English Library).

Another entertaining modern biography of Bismarck is refreshingly written, although it is not a straightforward chronological narrative and needs a basic knowledge and understanding of Bismarck's life for it to make sense. This is:

Edward Crankshaw, *Bismarck* (Macmillan 1981).

A very useful review of Bismarck's life and achievements in the light of modern historical research is:

Bruce Waller, *Bismarck* (Blackwell, 1985).

W. G. Shreeves, *Nationmaking in Nineteenth Century Europe* (Nelson, 1984) has been specifically written for A-Level students and contains extended discussion sections in which some issues are considered in great detail.

Sources on 'The Unification of Germany, 1815–90'

A huge amount of source material on the history of Germany in the nineteenth century has been published in English. The best place to begin the process of tracking down useful extracts for study at A-level is probably:
1   ed. **S. Brooks**, *Nineteenth Century Europe* (Macmillan, 1983).
   It is also worth looking at:
2   **Peter Jones** *The 1848 Revolutions* (Longman, 1981);
3   **W. G. Shreeves**, *Nationmaking in Nineteenth Century Europe* (Nelson, 1984); and
4   **A. Hewison**, *Bismarck and the Unification of Germany* (Edward Arnold, 1970); All of which contain a range of relevant sources, as well as information on larger and more specialist collections.
5   ed. **Asa Briggs**, *The Nineteenth Century*, (Thames and Hudson, 1970) contains a range of illustrations on the subject.

Acknowledgements

Acknowledgement is given for the use of extracts as follows:
Peter Jones, *The 1848 Revolutions*, pages 9–10, 12–13, 16, 27–8 (original source **Huber**, *Dokumente* Stuttgart, 1961)
ed **S. Brooks**, *Nineteenth Century Europe*, pages 26, 33, 35, 36
Snyder, *Blood and Iron Chancellor* (Van Nostrand, 1967), pages 51, 70 (reprinted in *Daily Telegraph*, August 4, 1898), 76, 90, 98–100
Wrighton and Cook, *Documents on World History, 1870–1918*, Macmillan, 1979, pages 74 (original source **Bismarck**, *Reminiscences*), 78–80
Grant Robertson, *Bismarck*, pages 74–5
Elliot, *Bismarck, Kaiser and Germany*, Longman, page 86
European Inheritance, OUP, 1956, page 95

The author and Publishers wish to thank the following for their permission to use copyright illustrations: The London Library/Bismarck 1915: page 50; The Mansell Collection: Cover (Emperor William I), page 78; Punch: page 98

The author and Publishers wish to thank the following examination boards for permission to include questions:
The Associated Examining Board; Joint Matriculation Board; Oxford and Cambridge Schools Examination Board; Southern Universities' Joint Board; University of Cambridge Local Examinations Syndicate; University of London School Examinations Department; University of Oxford Delegacy of Local Examinations; Welsh Joint Education Committee; Scottish Certificate of Education Examination Board. (The essay guidance sections are the responsibility of the General Editor and have not been approved by the Boards.)

Index